THE ATLAS OF SPACE

Jack Challoner

Consultant: James Muirden

Copper Beech Books
Brookfield, Connecticut

©Aladdin Books Ltd 2001

Produced by
Aladdin Books Ltd
28 Percy Street
London WIP 0LD

ISBN 0-7613-2157-8 (lib. bdg.)
ISBN 0-7613-2275-2 (pbk)

*First published in the
United States in 2001 by*
Copper Beech Books,
an imprint of
The Millbrook Press
2 Old New Milford Road
Brookfield, Connecticut 06804

Project Management
SGA design & illustration agency
Hadleigh
Suffolk IP7 5AP, UK

Project Manager
Philippa Jackaman (SGA)

Designer
Phil Kay

Editor
Linda Sonntag

Picture Research
Brian Hunter Smart

Illustrators
Geoff Ball
John Butler
Carol Daniel
Paul Doherty
Piers Harper
Colin Howard
Mike Lacey
Stuart Lees
Alex Pang
Stan Peach
Richard Rockwood
Stephen Sweet
Mike Taylor
Simon Tegg
Ian Thompson
Catherine Ward

Printed in Belgium

Cataloging-in-Publication data is
on file at the Library of Congress.

The author, Jack Challoner, has
written more than twenty books
on science and technology for all
ages. His favorite scientific subject
is astronomy. He also writes and
presents scientific shows in
schools and museums.

The consultant, James Muirden, has
written many books for children and
adults about astronomy and how to
observe the sky. In 1964, he founded
The Astronomer, an international
magazine for amateur observers.

CONTENTS

INTRODUCTION

Space is what you gaze into when you look up on a clear night, but it is also where we live. Our planet, Earth, is a huge ball of rock that hurtles through space, circling a star that we call the Sun. There are other planets, too, and other stars. Thanks to the sciences called astronomy and astrophysics, we now understand much of what is in space. But there are many mysteries yet to solve.

Planet Earth is one of nine planets that travel around, or orbit, the Sun. Earth orbits in a near-perfect circle about 93 million miles (150 million km) from the Sun. It takes our planet one year to complete each orbit, traveling at a speed of 67,000 miles per hour (108,000 km/h). The Sun is one of billions of stars which together make up the Milky Way Galaxy, and the Milky Way is one of billions of galaxies to be found in all of space—the Universe—which is a very large place indeed.

Planet Earth

Light from the Sun hits Earth, leaving one side in shadow. Sunlight is white light: a mixture of all the colors of the spectrum. Nitrogen gas in the atmosphere scatters some of the blue light in all directions—including back out into space. This is why our world looks so blue from space. Clouds and large areas of ice reflect all the colors in sunlight, so they appear white. The atmosphere is a layer of gases only about 125 miles (200 km) thick. It does more than just give Earth its colorful look: it supports life. No living things have yet been found on other planets.

▲ The nine planets of the Solar System orbit the Sun. The two largest planets are Jupiter (right) and Saturn (left).

Solar System

Earth is one of nine planets that orbit the Sun. Together with millions of chunks of ice and dust called comets and lumps of rock called meteoroids, the Sun and the planets make up the Solar System. The distance from the center of the Solar System to its edge is huge: light takes about five hours to travel from the Sun to Pluto, the planet farthest from the Sun. But the Solar System extends far beyond the orbit of Pluto: there are millions of comets in orbit around the Sun, much, much farther out. Beyond the Solar System, space is empty—except for very thin traces of gas—over vast distances. The nearest star after our Sun is so far away that its light takes four years to reach us.

▲ Earth is the most colorful planet in the Solar System, and a very special place.

To understand how vast the Universe is, it is useful to think about how long light takes to reach us from stars, other planets, and other galaxies. Light travels 186,000 miles every second (300,000 km/s). At that speed, you could cross the Atlantic Ocean in about one hundredth of a second and travel around the world in just over a tenth of a second. The nearest thing to us in space is the Moon. Light from the Moon takes just over one second to reach us. Light from the Sun takes more than eight minutes, but even the distance from the Sun to Earth is tiny compared to the rest of the Universe.

▲ The spiral Milky Way Galaxy is a flat disk, with a bulge in the center.

▲ Galaxies are like islands in the vast empty ocean of the Universe. They are all unimaginably far away.

The Milky Way Galaxy

Nearly all of the individual stars we can see in the night sky are members of the Milky Way Galaxy: a huge, flat, rotating spiral shape made up of about 200 billion stars. The Solar System—situated in one of the spiral arms fairly near to the edge—takes about 220 million years to go around once. Light takes about 100,000 years to travel from one edge of the Milky Way Galaxy to the opposite edge. To help you imagine the size of the galaxy, imagine the whole Solar System the size of a small coin. On that scale, the galaxy would be about the size of the entire USA. Outside our galaxy, in intergalactic space, there is virtually nothing—until you come to another galaxy, far, far away.

The Universe

Light takes over two million years to reach us from the nearest big galaxy outside our own. There are countless other galaxies throughout space, all separated by huge distances. They are clustered together, with even greater distances between the clusters. Light reaching us from as far as we can see—what astronomers call the edge of the observable Universe—takes a staggering 12 billion years. When you think about the entire Universe, Earth seems a very, very tiny place.

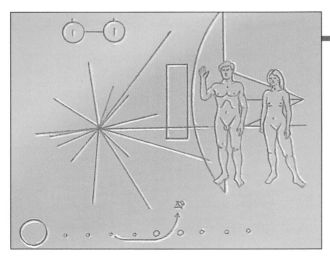

Message to the Universe

The Universe is so vast that it seems likely that life exists elsewhere. If it does, extraterrestrials (living things not from Earth) may one day come across this plaque, which was attached to a spacecraft launched into space in 1972. It shows a man and a woman standing next to the spacecraft, a map of the Solar System, and a diagram showing the Sun's position relative to other notable objects in space. It is extremely unlikely that it will ever be found.

◀ This plaque was attached to a spacecraft called *Pioneer 10*, which traveled past the planets Mars and Jupiter before heading away from the Solar System. You can see the path of the spacecraft from the diagram at the bottom of the plaque.

WHERE ARE WE?

Together with the Sun, our nearest neighbors in space are the eight other planets of the Solar System which orbit the Sun. The planets are much closer than the stars and appear to shift their position night by night against the background of stars. In fact, the word "planet" comes from a Greek word meaning "wanderers."

Of the nine planets, only Mercury, Venus, Mars, and Jupiter are visible from Earth without the aid of a telescope, so the remaining planets have only been discovered since the invention of the telescope about 400 years ago. Pluto was discovered as recently as 1930. The four planets closest to the Sun are called the terrestrial (Earthlike) planets, because, like Earth, they are relatively small and are made mainly of rock. The next four are much larger and are made mainly of gases. Astronomers often refer to them as the gas giants or Jovian (Jupiterlike) planets. Most of the planets have an outer layer of gases called an atmosphere, held to the planet by gravity—the same force that keeps us on the ground.

Using telescopes, astronomers can pick out a planet's surface details and also work out its composition (what it is made of). The best way to discover more about the planets is to pay them a visit. So far, people have not stood on any other planets, but we have sent robot spacecraft, called space probes, to investigate on our behalf. Much of what we know about the planets has come from photographs and other data gathered by space probes.

▶ Shown here are the main constituents of the Solar System: the Sun and the nine planets. The relative sizes of the Sun and the planets are correct, and the planets are shown in their correct order out from the Sun, but the distances involved—from each other and from the Sun—are not shown to scale.

1 Mercury

Closest to the Sun is a small rocky planet called Mercury. It is not much larger than our Moon and has a similar surface, pockmarked with craters left behind as rocks and comets crashed into the planet early in the history of the Solar System. The Sun blasts Mercury with heat and light and other forms of radiation, making it a very inhospitable place.

2 Venus

Visiting Venus would be very hazardous. The planet's atmosphere is so thick that it traps heat like a greenhouse, giving Venus the hottest surface of any planet in the Solar System. There is no liquid water, and the atmosphere contains clouds of deadly sulfuric acid, so Venus is a dry and poisonous world.

Sun

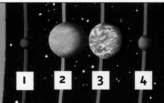

| 1 | 2 | 3 | 4 |

3 Earth

Our home planet is remarkable. It is one of the few places in the Solar System that has liquid water. In fact, more than two-thirds of the planet's surface is covered with it. The liquid water—mainly in the oceans—together with the atmosphere helps to stabilize the planet's temperature and sustain a rich diversity of life.

4 Mars

Astronomers often call Mars "the Red Planet." This is because the rocks and dust on its surface have a high proportion of iron oxide, the main chemical in rust. Mars has polar ice caps that contain water ice and frozen carbon dioxide and has strong winds that constantly whip up dust storms.

5 Jupiter

With a diameter about 11 times that of Earth, Jupiter is by far the largest planet in the Solar System. It is composed almost entirely of gases—mainly hydrogen and helium—but it has a small, rocky core surrounded by liquid hydrogen. One of the most striking features of Jupiter is a huge storm twice the size of Earth, called the Great Red Spot.

7 Uranus

The color of Uranus is due to a gas called methane in the upper atmosphere, which reflects only blue light. Beneath the thick atmosphere is a layer of ice particles floating in a mixture of gases, and at the center lies a large, rocky core. Uranus was the first planet to be discovered using a telescope—it is not visible to the naked eye.

9 Pluto

Little is known about Pluto, which is the smallest planet in the Solar System. We do know that it is a cold, rocky body with a moon that is nearly half the size of the planet itself. For most of its 248-year orbit, Pluto is the planet farthest from the Sun, but its irregular path around the Sun takes it inside Neptune's orbit for several years at a time.

5

6

7

8

9

6 Saturn

The second-largest planet in the Solar System is Saturn. Like all the gas giants, it has a series of rings around it, made of chunks of ice and rock. The rings of Saturn are the most spectacular of any planet and are visible even with a small telescope. Saturn is the planet with the most moons—30 have been found so far.

8 Neptune

The last of the gas giants is Neptune. It is very similar to Uranus, but slightly smaller. The violent winds in Neptune's deep atmosphere—the strongest in the whole Solar System—blow at more than 680 miles per hour (1,100 km/h). The tops of the gas clouds are featureless, and there remains much to be learned about this distant world.

OUR HOME PLANET

Planet Earth is beautiful. Every morning, without fail, the Sun rises in the eastern sky, and every evening it sets in the western sky. The changing seasons bring with them cycles of birth, death, and renewal. Parts of the world are hot and other parts are cold. There are forests and mountains, birds and fish, and we humans are here to appreciate it. But Earth has not always been this way.

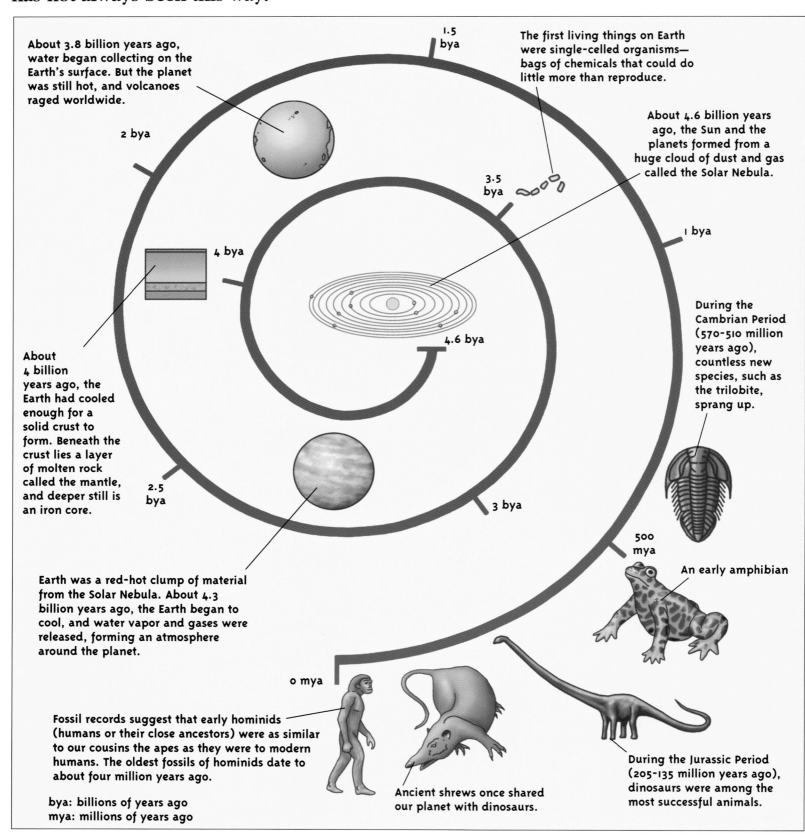

About 3.8 billion years ago, water began collecting on the Earth's surface. But the planet was still hot, and volcanoes raged worldwide.

The first living things on Earth were single-celled organisms—bags of chemicals that could do little more than reproduce.

About 4.6 billion years ago, the Sun and the planets formed from a huge cloud of dust and gas called the Solar Nebula.

About 4 billion years ago, the Earth had cooled enough for a solid crust to form. Beneath the crust lies a layer of molten rock called the mantle, and deeper still is an iron core.

During the Cambrian Period (570-510 million years ago), countless new species, such as the trilobite, sprang up.

Earth was a red-hot clump of material from the Solar Nebula. About 4.3 billion years ago, the Earth began to cool, and water vapor and gases were released, forming an atmosphere around the planet.

An early amphibian

Fossil records suggest that early hominids (humans or their close ancestors) were as similar to our cousins the apes as they were to modern humans. The oldest fossils of hominids date to about four million years ago.

bya: billions of years ago
mya: millions of years ago

Ancient shrews once shared our planet with dinosaurs.

During the Jurassic Period (205-135 million years ago), dinosaurs were among the most successful animals.

1.5 bya · 2 bya · 3.5 bya · 1 bya · 4 bya · 4.6 bya · 2.5 bya · 3 bya · 500 mya · 0 mya

▲ Scientists have worked to piece together Earth's long history. Geologists, who study rocks, and space scientists have concluded that the Solar System was probably born from a huge cloud of dust and gas, which collapsed to form the Sun and planets. Biologists, who study living things, and paleontologists, who study fossils, are learning how life developed, from simple organisms to complex plants and animals.

Planet Earth was created when the Solar System was born, more than four billion years ago. There are no photographs of the early Earth, and no one was around to tell us about it, but scientists have many clues to help them build up a picture of the long history of our planet. For example, fossils tell us what kind of plants and animals inhabited the Earth long ago. From the fossil record, scientists have learned that life first appeared on Earth about 3.8 billion years ago, and that it developed by a long, slow process of evolution. By studying rocks deep in the ground and in the seabed, geologists can discover what forces have shaped the landscape and even how the gases of the atmosphere have changed. The Sun plays an important role in shaping the Earth. Without it, our planet would be a cold and barren place. The Sun gives us day and night, the seasons, and the energy to stay alive.

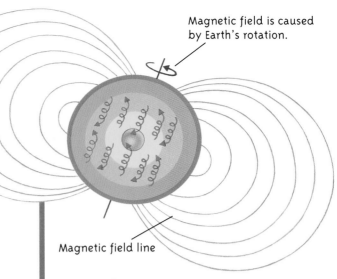

Magnetic field is caused by Earth's rotation.

Magnetic field line

▲ Earth's magnetism is produced by the planet's iron core. The core spins at a different rate from the rest of the planet, and this generates strong electric currents that produce the magnetic field.

Earth's invisible force field

Like all the planets, Earth behaves like an enormous magnet. Just as a magnet has two poles—north and south—the Earth has a magnetic north and a magnetic south, where the magnetic forces are concentrated. The Earth's magnetic poles are found close to the geographical poles—the top and bottom of the Earth. The magnetism forms a force field called the magnetosphere in the local space environment. Scientists visualize the force field by drawing lines that show the direction of the magnetic forces, as in the diagram above.

◀ The orbits of the Earth around the Sun, and the Moon around the Earth (not to scale). Each takes one year to journey around the Sun, and one day to rotate (spin) once. The Sun gives us light during the day.

Days, months, and years

Each revolution (orbit) of Earth around the Sun takes $365\frac{1}{4}$ Earth days. The quarter of a day each year makes up a whole day every four years—February 29th in each leap year. Like all the planets, Earth rotates (spins) as it revolves around the Sun. It takes 23 hours, 56 minutes, 4 seconds to rotate once, but because it moves through space too, it takes four minutes longer—24 hours—to face the Sun again. Our word "month" is based on the Moon's motion around the Earth: the Moon takes about $27\frac{1}{4}$ days to revolve around the Earth.

Curtains of light

A stream of particles called the solar wind arrives at Earth at high speed. The particles are attracted down toward the North Pole and the South Pole, where they produce dramatic light displays, called auroras, in the skies of the polar regions. In the north, they are called the northern lights and in the south, the southern lights. When the Sun is very active, with energetic events occurring on its surface, the solar wind is stronger and the auroras are much brighter. A strong solar wind can also affect satellite communications and can even cause power cuts on Earth.

▼ The color of an aurora depends on the energy of the particles in the solar wind. Green light means higher energy particles than red light, for example.

HISTORY OF SPACE

The stars, planets, and other objects in space existed long before there were people to look at them. People in the very earliest civilizations invented myths to account for the lights they saw in the sky. Later, astronomers worked out theories attempting to explain the motions of the Sun, Moon, stars, and planets.

Neither the myths nor the early theories were correct, but they lasted for thousands of years. In the 1600s, new mathematics, together with the invention of the telescope, allowed people to develop new ideas and make new discoveries. It was not until the 1800s that astronomers finally began to understand what the stars are made of, and just how far away they are.

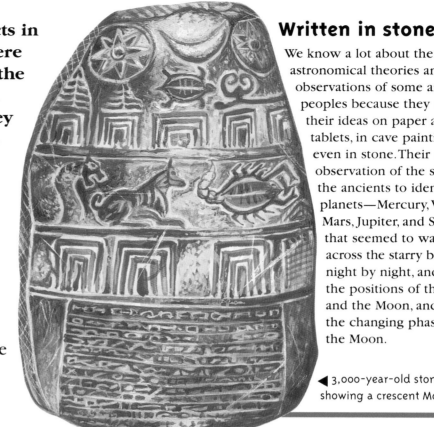

Written in stone

We know a lot about the astronomical theories and observations of some ancient peoples because they recorded their ideas on paper and clay tablets, in cave paintings, and even in stone. Their careful observation of the sky led the ancients to identify five planets—Mercury, Venus, Mars, Jupiter, and Saturn— that seemed to wander across the starry background night by night, and to chart the positions of the Sun and the Moon, and record the changing phases of the Moon.

◀ 3,000-year-old stone tablet showing a crescent Moon

Ancient calendars

Astronomers in ancient Egypt and in the ancient civilization of Mesopotamia were among the first to use patterns in the movements of the Sun, the Moon, and the stars to keep track of days, months, and years. Certain times of the year—when the Sun was at its highest, or a particular star made its first appearance of the year—were important. By charting the seasons, people would know when to plant their crops. Many civilizations worshiped the Sun and the Moon, and believed they could help predict the future.

The wrong idea

The idea that the Earth is at the center of the Universe was developed in ancient Greece. For a long time people continued to believe that the Sun, the Moon, the planets, and even the stars traveled around the Earth. The Earth-centered, or geocentric, theory did explain the motions of celestial objects (objects in the sky) fairly well, which is one reason why people held on to it. Another is that many people believed the Earth deserved a special place in the Universe—right at the center.

▲▶ Stonehenge, in southern England, was built about 5,000 years ago, probably to help people worship the Sun.

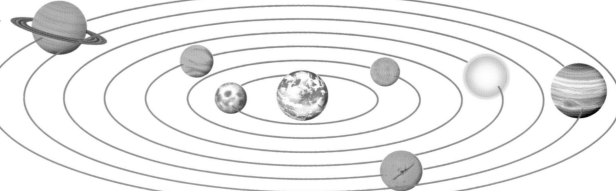

▶ The geocentric Universe, with the Earth at the center

Putting it right

One of the great thinkers of the Renaissance was a Polish astronomer called Nicolaus Copernicus. In 1543, Copernicus published his heliocentric theory, which put the Sun at the center of the Universe. The invention of the telescope—early in the 1600s—provided evidence in favor of the heliocentric theory. In 1609, for example, Italian astronomer Galileo Galilei gazed at Jupiter through his telescope and discovered four moons that go around the planet in a way that fitted exactly with Copernicus's theory. He also discovered that the planets Venus and Mercury have phases like our Moon. This showed that they are closer to the Sun than Earth is—impossible if Earth is at the center.

▶ Galileo Galilei made many sensational discoveries with his homemade telescope.

◀ Isaac Newton (1643-1727) first explained universal gravity, the force that binds the Universe together.

Big thinker

In 1709, English scientist Isaac Newton published his Theory of Universal Gravitation, which explained exactly how the planets move around the Sun in terms of the force of gravity. Newton's theory was successful in helping to prove that the geocentric theory of the Universe was wrong. For the first time, astronomers could begin to work out the masses, speeds, and distances of the planets, and predict their movements with great accuracy.

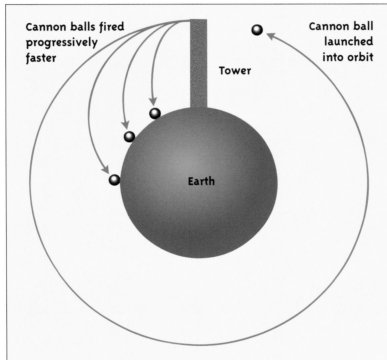

Cannon balls fired progressively faster

Tower

Cannon ball launched into orbit

Earth

Gravity and orbits

Newton realized that the same force that gives objects weight here on Earth attracts (pulls together) everything in the Universe. He showed how his theory of gravity could explain the orbits of the planets and the Moon by discussing an object fired horizontally from the top of a tall tower. If the object is fired only slowly, it will fall to the ground in a curved path. But if it is fired fast enough, that curved path will exactly match the curvature of the Earth, and the object will be in orbit.

Colorful ideas

Newton's theory was the beginning of modern astronomy. Another very important development was spectroscopy—a way of identifying chemical elements by the light they give off when they are hot. In the 1800s, scientists heated elements in laboratories and analyzed the light by passing it through a prism to produce a spectrum. Astronomers found characteristic patterns in the spectrum of light from the Sun and the stars, which enabled them to work out what stars are made of. In 1898, they observed new lines in the Sun's spectrum. This meant that they had discovered a new element. They called it helium, after *helios*, the Greek word for the Sun.

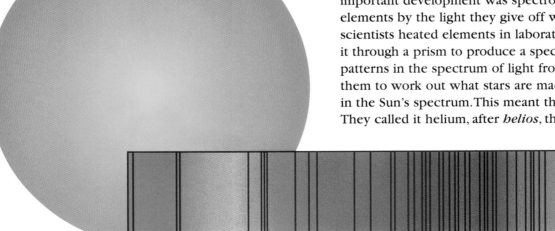

◀ Sunlight contains information that tells astronomers what chemical elements are present in the Sun. The same is true for other stars.

WATCHING THE SKY

A starry sky looks like a solid black background dotted with thousands of tiny lights. Ancient peoples tried to make sense of the random arrangement of stars by identifying patterns, called constellations, and giving them names from mythology.

The stars are so far away that they stay in the same positions—relative to each other—from night to night, and even over hundreds of years. So the same constellations that the ancients devised are still used today. Once you are familiar with some of them, you can begin to find your way around the night sky. Many of the early astronomers thought the sky really was a solid background—a huge round sphere, called the celestial sphere, with the Earth at its center. They believed that the celestial sphere was gently turning, causing the stars to rise, move across the sky, and set. The Sun, Moon, and planets do move relative to the "fixed" stars, and so the ancients believed that these objects orbited the Earth in perfect circles inside the celestial sphere. We now know that the rising and setting of all the objects in the sky is due to the rotation of planet Earth, and that the background of the sky is simply the blackness of space.

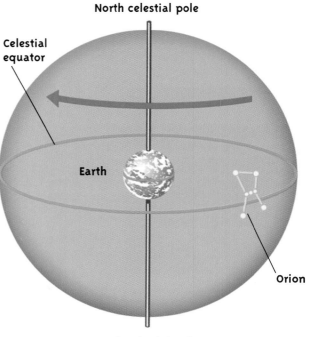

▶ The constellation of Orion, shown on the imaginary celestial sphere

Mapping the stars

The constellations move across the sky each night, as if the celestial sphere were turning, with an axis through the north and south. The celestial sphere does not exist, and it is the rotation of planet Earth that causes the constellations to move across the sky.

A different view

Early astronomers believed that the stars existed on the inner surface of the celestial sphere, or that they were holes letting in light from heaven. But stars in a constellation are not close together in space: they simply appear close, seen from Earth. Constellations do not contain stars that are related, and there is no celestial sphere, but modern astronomers still use these ideas to map the sky.

▼ The constellation Orion, as seen from a point in space far from Earth. You can see that most of the stars in Orion have nothing to do with each other.

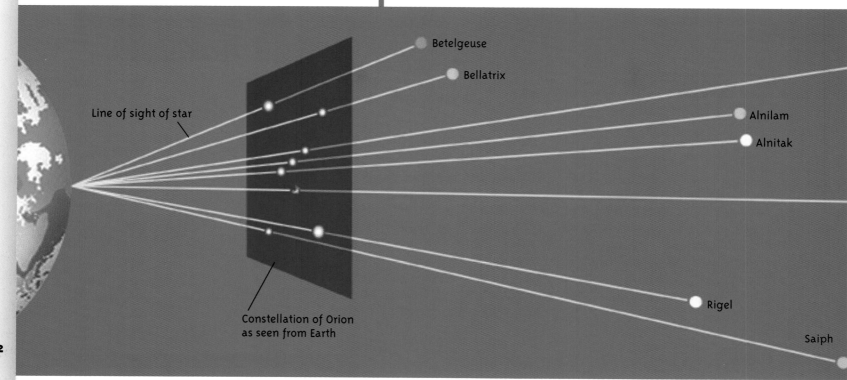

Line of sight of star

Constellation of Orion as seen from Earth

Betelgeuse

Bellatrix

Alnilam

Alnitak

Rigel

Saiph

The whirling sky

If you leave the shutter of a camera open, pointing to the sky for about an hour on a really clear night, the result should be a photograph like this one. The stars did not move in circles while the shutter was open; the camera spun around because it was on the rotating Earth. The star at the middle is directly above Earth's North Pole —at the north celestial pole—and so does not appear to move with the others.

◀ Star trails left during a long-exposure photo of the northern sky at night. The Pole Star, Polaris, is the bright star at the center.

▲ Time-lapse picture of the Sun's apparent movement during one day

The moving Sun

Like the stars, the Sun, Moon, and planets also appear to move across the sky because of the rotation of the Earth. The Earth turns west to east, so the Sun moves east to west across the sky. This picture shows how the Sun moves from sunrise to sunset. The Sun's highest point varies during the year. It is lower in the sky during the winter than during the summer.

A year in space

At each point of Earth's one-year orbit, we see the Sun against a different part of the sky. The daytime sky is too bright to see the stars, but they are still there. The constellations that the Sun appears to blaze through in the course of a year are called the Zodiac. The actual line that the Sun follows through the sky is called the ecliptic.

▶ The Zodiac constellations on the celestial sphere

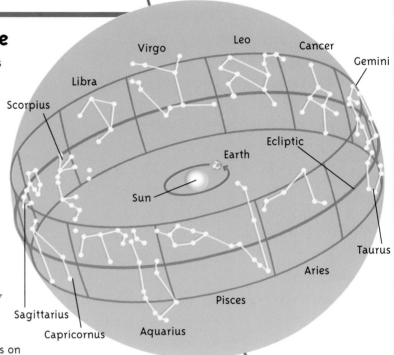

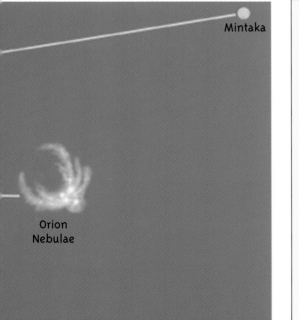

Mintaka

Orion Nebulae

The Zodiac

The Sun's path as seen from Earth passes through these 12 constellations. They may be familiar to you as the Signs of the Zodiac.

 Aries (The Ram)   Libra (The Scales)

 Taurus (The Bull)   Scorpius (The Scorpion)

 Gemini (The Twins)   Sagittarius (The Archer)

 Cancer (The Crab)   Capricornus (The Goat)

 Leo (The Lion)   Aquarius (The Water Carrier)

 Virgo (The Virgin)   Pisces (The Fish)

The sky has changed slightly since the ancient Greeks worked out the Zodiac, so the Sun appears to pass through one more constellation, Andromeda.

FINDING THE STARS

If you were standing at the North Pole on a starry night with a clear view of the horizon all around you, you would see half the celestial sphere; if you did the same at the South Pole, you would see the other half. From anywhere else on Earth, you can see some of the constellations in each of the hemispheres.

Astronomers use maps of the two celestial hemispheres (half-spheres) to find their way around the sky. Since our planet orbits the Sun, the position of the Sun in the celestial sphere gradually shifts during the year. The part of the sky where the Sun is, is so bright that the constellations in that region of the celestial hemisphere are not visible. So exactly which constellations you can see on any particular night depends upon the time of year. In the sky, all stars appear as points of light—even through a telescope. On star maps, however, the stars are shown as dots of different sizes—the brighter a star, the bigger the dot. The same is true of photographs of stars: when bright light falls onto a photographic film, it affects the film, spreading out to form a larger dot.

◀ The northern celestial hemisphere. A star called Polaris (the Pole Star) sits close to the celestial pole.

The names of the constellations are in capitals, the names of the stars are in normal type.

Bright stars

The brightness of an object in the sky is called its magnitude. Strangely, the brighter a star, the lower its magnitude. So a star of magnitude 2 is brighter than a star of magnitude 3. Stars of magnitude 6 are just visible with the naked eye on a very clear, dark night. Really bright stars have magnitudes that are less than zero. The brightest star in the night sky, for example, is called Sirius, and has a magnitude of -1.4. The brightest star of all is our Sun, which has a magnitude of -26.7.

▶ Photograph showing the constellation of Orion and Canis Major. The brightest star is Sirius.

▲ Through a powerful telescope, the Andromeda Galaxy is a spectacular sight. This is how our own Milky Way Galaxy would look from the outside.

Looking at other galaxies

All of the stars that appear on these maps are in our galaxy. Some maps also show the other galaxies. Although galaxies contain billions of stars, they are so far away that only a few are bright enough to be seen without a telescope. With a magnitude of 3.4, the Andromeda Galaxy—in the constellation of Andromeda—is one of them. It is the most distant object visible to the naked eye, and appears as a small hazy patch of light. Two small, relatively nearby galaxies— the Large and Small Magellanic Clouds—are quite prominent in the southern celestial hemisphere.

▼ The sky in and around the constellation of Sagittarius is filled with thousands of faint stars.

▼ The southern celestial hemisphere. The three brightest stars—Sirius, Canopus, and Alpha Centauri—are in this part of the sky.

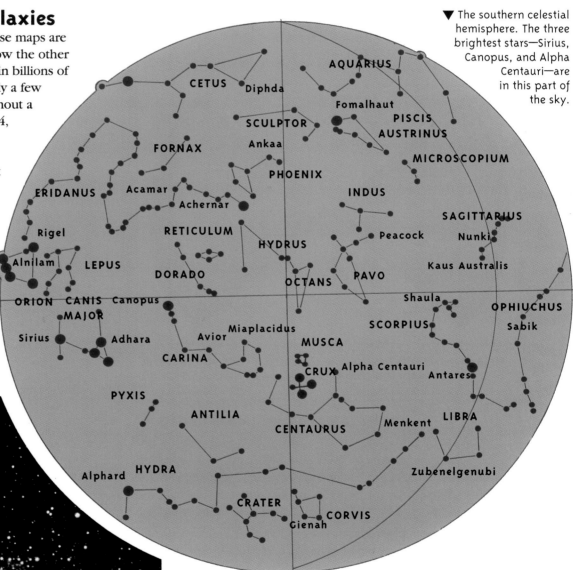

Galactic center

Our galaxy is like an island in the vast empty sea of space. The Solar System is near the edge of the galaxy, so we see many more stars when we look in the direction of the galactic center than when we look in the opposite direction. The galactic center lies in the constellation of Sagittarius, an area of the sky so rich in stars that it appears milky white—hence the name "Milky Way." If you look at this part of the sky with binoculars, you will see many stars that are invisible to the naked eye.

TELESCOPES

WATCHING THE SKY

Before the telescope was invented, astronomers had only their eyes to help them search for answers to their questions about space. The invention of the telescope in 1608 opened up a new world in the night sky, giving astronomers a chance to discover new planets, galaxies, and millions of previously unseen stars, and to find out more about what space is really like.

Telescopes have many advantages over eyes. Most people know that telescopes can make objects look bigger—as if they are closer than they really are. This is magnification. Telescopes can collect much more light than eyes—and therefore see much fainter objects. This is because they can have an aperture (hole through which light passes) that is much larger than the pupil of an eye. Telescopes are perhaps most effective of all when they are used with cameras. Photography produces a permanent record of observations and provides a way of collecting light over long periods, so that really faint objects become visible. One more important property of telescopes is their resolving power. This is the ability to see stars that are very close together as separate points of light, where the human eye blurs them together.

▼ A refracting telescope, with an objective lens and an eyepiece

Refracting telescopes

Some telescopes use only lenses to produce images. They are refracting telescopes, and have a large lens (the objective) to collect light and produce an image inside the telescope tube, and a smaller lens (the eyepiece) to view the image. In most refracting telescopes, the objective lens is made up of two lenses. This gets rid of chromatic aberration—the colored fringes around an image that are present with a single objective lens.

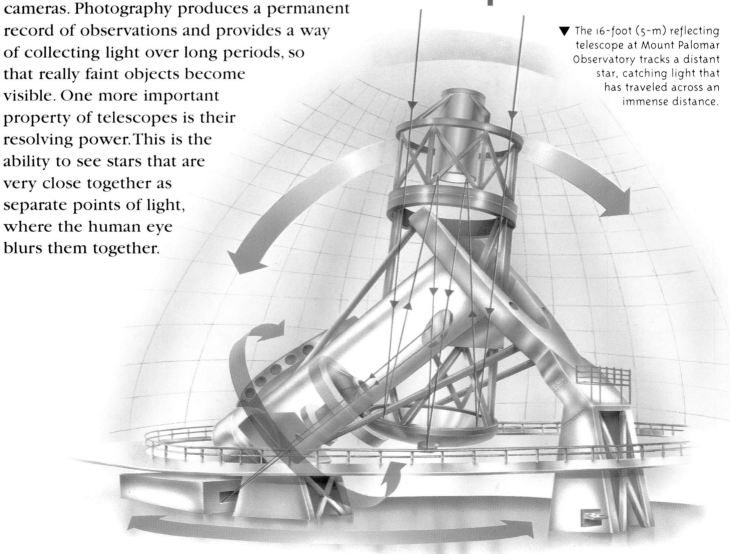

▼ The 16-foot (5-m) reflecting telescope at Mount Palomar Observatory tracks a distant star, catching light that has traveled across an immense distance.

Following the stars

Most telescopes are mounted in such a way that they can be moved easily to find any object in the sky quickly. Many also have mechanisms that slowly move the telescope's mounting (base support) to compensate for the Earth's rotation. If a mounting does not do this, a star moves quickly across the field of view of a powerful telescope, since the telescope magnifies the slow drift of a distant object caused by the Earth's rotation, as well as the object itself.

Reflecting telescopes

A curved mirror—rather than a lens—is used to collect and focus light in a reflecting telescope. In a type of reflecting telescope called a Newtonian reflector, the light bounces off a small, flat mirror inside the tube to be magnified and viewed through a small eyepiece lens at the side of the telescope. Other types of reflector have different arrangements of mirrors. More light is lost passing through a lens than reflecting off a mirror—so a reflecting telescope is generally better than a refracting telescope.

◄ A Newtonian reflector with a mounting that makes it easy to track stars as they drift across the sky

Electronic imaging

At the back of a human eye is a screen called the retina, which is covered with millions of light-sensitive cells that send messages to the brain. Most modern professional telescopes have a similar screen, called a CCD (charge-coupled device), which has millions of light-sensitive squares on its surface. Each square sends messages to a computer, which displays or analyzes the image. The more squares on the CCD, the better the resolving power of the telescope.

▶ An image from a telescope— made of millions of tiny squares

Professional telescopes

Most professional telescopes are reflectors. The larger the mirror, the brighter the image and the better the resolution of the telescope. There is a limit to the size of a single mirror, so since the 1970s, some telescopes have been built with multiple mirrors that work together to produce the equivalent of one huge mirror. The Very Large Telescope in Chile will soon become the largest telescope in the world. Its four 27-foot (8.2-m) mirrors will be as powerful as a single 52-foot (16-m) mirror. There is even a plan to build a 52-foot mirror. If it goes ahead, this OverWhelmingly Large telescope (OWL) will begin operation in about 2016.

▼ Mauna Kea, Hawaii. The observatories are clustered together high on mountains.

Correcting the wobble

The atmosphere is filled with pockets of air that jostle around as warm and cool air mix. This affects the light that passes through it, causing stars to twinkle. Through powerful telescopes, stars do not only twinkle: they appear to wobble. To reduce the wobble, most large observatories are sited high on mountains, where the air is less turbulent and the starlight passes through less of the atmosphere. The Keck 33-foot (10-m) reflector has 36 mirrors that are constantly adjusted by computer to correct the wobble.

▼ Inside the dome of the Keck telescope at Mauna Kea, Hawaii

Some record-making telescopes

1609-10 Sensational findings in Italy with Galileo's 2-inch (50-mm) telescope (the "Old Discoverer")

1668 Isaac Newton (England) makes the first reflecting telescope with a mirror about 1 inch (25 mm) across

1789 William Herschel (England) builds a 3.9-foot (1.2-m) reflecting telescope

1845 William Parsons (Ireland) builds a 5.9-foot (1.8-m) reflector

1917 George Ellery Hale builds an 8.2-foot (2.5-m) reflector at Mount Wilson, California

1948 A 16.4-foot (5-m) reflector (also Hale's creation) is completed at Mount Palomar, California

▲ A 14-foot reflecting telescope

1991 Keck I, a 32.8-foot (10-m) reflector with multiple mirrors is installed at Mauna Kea, Hawaii; Keck II added in 1997

2001 The Very Large Telescope (VLT), using four 26.9-foot (8.2-m) telescopes linked together, Cerro Paranal, Chile

INVISIBLE RAYS FROM SPACE

WATCHING THE SKY

Most telescopes collect only light from distant objects in space—they are called optical telescopes. But light is only one of a number of types of electromagnetic radiation. Radio waves, infrared, ultraviolet, X-rays, and gamma rays are the others. Most stars and galaxies emit (give out) other types of radiation too, and detecting these can provide huge amounts of information about space.

All objects produce electromagnetic radiation. The type of radiation depends upon the temperature of the object—a very useful fact when astronomers want to find out the temperature of a distant star. The coolest objects emit only weak radio waves; warmer objects produce infrared, too. Hotter still, and objects glow with visible light. Very hot objects produce ultraviolet and even X-rays. The very hottest objects may even produce gamma rays. Electromagnetic radiation is also produced by other processes. Radio waves can be produced by electrically charged particles called electrons moving quickly back and forth. X-rays are produced by electrons losing huge amounts of energy very quickly, while gamma rays are produced by high-energy processes deep inside the nucleus (central part) of an atom. All these processes happen in stars and galaxies, and astronomers can detect the radiation by using specially designed telescopes.

▶ Visible light and radio waves are the main forms of electromagnetic radiation that pass through the atmosphere.

Across the spectrum

Electromagnetic radiation travels both as waves—like ripples on water—and as particles, like balls. Electromagnetic waves can have short or long wavelengths. The various types of radiation form a continuous spectrum (range) —from short-wavelength gamma rays to long-wavelength radio waves. Across the entire electromagnetic spectrum, only visible light and radio waves pass through Earth's atmosphere well enough to be of use to ground-based astronomers.

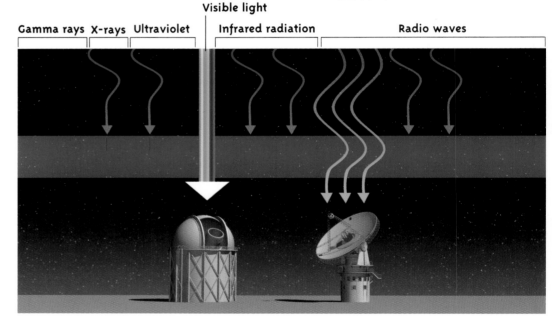

Visible light

Gamma rays · X-rays · Ultraviolet · Infrared radiation · Radio waves

Tuning in to the Universe

Many objects in space emit radio waves. Radio telescopes detect the waves with dishes like those on a satellite television receiver. Just as starlight is dimmer the farther away you are from the star, radio waves from space are very weak by the time they reach Earth. So the larger a telescope's dish, the better. The largest movable dish, at Effelsberg in Germany, has a diameter of 328 feet (100 m). The biggest dish of all is on the Arecibo Radio Telescope. It is 1,000 feet (305 m) in diameter, but can't be moved around, so astronomers cannot choose what they want to see.

◀ The Arecibo Radio Telescope was built into a natural hollow on the island of Puerto Rico.

▲ The Very Large Array in New Mexico has 27 82-foot (25-m) dishes. Together, they act as a single dish 22 miles (36 km) across.

Working together

By combining the signals from an array of several radio telescopes, astronomers can synthesize a single, much larger dish. The signals from all the radio telescopes in an array are combined by computer, and the result is an incredibly detailed picture. The farther apart the individual telescopes, the more detailed is the image. Another way to synthesize a very large dish is to monitor a single object in the sky for several hours. This is Earth-rotation synthesis, where a few dishes spread across the globe can act as a single huge dish, as the Earth rotates.

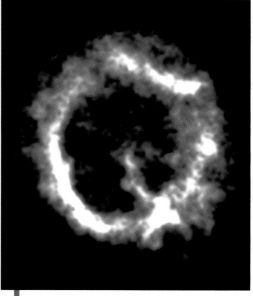
▲ An image from an orbiting X-ray telescope showing a shell of gas around a dying star. The star itself is too dim to be seen by optical telescopes.

What do radio telescopes see?

Computers connected to radio telescope dishes produce radio maps of small regions of the sky. Galaxies and individual stars produce radio waves, and even planet Jupiter is a strong radio source. The gas and dust between the stars also emit radio waves. Many discoveries have been made using radio telescopes, including energetic galaxies, in which electrons are trapped in powerful magnetic fields. It is illegal to broadcast radio waves that radio telescopes can detect, but even so, mobile telephones and other radio sources can interfere with radio telescope observations.

▶ The very bright object in this group of remote galaxies is a quasar—an extremely distant, energetic galaxy. Quasars are powerful radio sources.

Telescopes in orbit

We need to put telescopes above the atmosphere if we want to detect electromagnetic radiation other than light or radio waves coming from space. That means launching telescopes into space on rockets. An American rocket was the first to carry X-ray instruments into space in 1962. The first orbiting gamma ray observatory was launched in 1969, and the first orbiting ultraviolet observatory in 1972. The Sun is a powerful source of ultraviolet light and X-rays as well as visible light, and in the 1990s, several space telescopes were launched that point only at the Sun. The Hubble Space Telescope is an orbiting observatory that carries both an optical telescope and an infrared telescope.

Signs of life

If extraterrestrials want to get in touch with us, they may use radio waves. Since 1960, radio telescopes have been used to search the sky for unusual signals. In 1967, astronomer Jocelyn Bell Burnell detected regular pulses of radio waves that she thought might have come from an extraterrestrial civilization. In fact, she had discovered the first known pulsar, a rapidly spinning, dying star. We earthlings have also sent out our own radio signals: in 1974 and 1999, coded messages were sent as powerful bursts of radio waves.

▲ Will ET phone us?

The search goes on

There is no reason to suppose that life would develop only on our planet, and many astronomers think that the existence of extraterrestrial intelligent life is very likely. The Search for Extraterrestrial Intelligence (SETI) is an international effort to detect signals from civilizations in outer space. It gathers information from radio telescopes, including the enormous dish at Arecibo. Part of the effort is a project called SETI@home, which uses personal computers across the world to look for clues.

▲ Searching for ET at home

THE HUBBLE SPACE TELESCOPE

WATCHING THE SKY

Imagine spending your life peering through a dirty window, then one day being able to see the world clearly for the first time. That is how astronomers feel about the Hubble Space Telescope. This remarkable instrument has given astronomers crystal-clear glimpses of the Universe, and is helping them to solve all sorts of riddles about space.

The Hubble Space Telescope (HST) is able to produce extremely sharp images because it is high above the atmosphere—in orbit around planet Earth. The atmosphere allows us to see out into space fairly well, but the air is constantly moving around. So ground-based observations of space can never be perfectly clear. The Hubble Space Telescope—about as big as a tanker truck—was launched in 1990. Since then, it has beamed thousands of spectacular images back to Earth. Among them are an image of the most distant object ever photographed, amazing pictures of star birth in distant clouds of gas, and some of the best-ever pictures of faraway galaxies. It has also found evidence of massive black holes and given scientists clues to the biggest mystery of all: how old is the Universe?

▼ Rear view of the Hubble Space Telescope. The solar panels are the two large, flat pieces on either side of the telescope tube. The main mirror (yellow) and scientific instruments are housed in the rear section, shown here detached for clarity.

Main mirror and scientific instruments

▲ The 7.8-foot (2.4-m) mirror stands on its turntable while the surface is being polished.

Instruments aboard the HST

1 The Wide Field and Planetary Camera (WFPC2)—a high-resolution digital camera.

2 Space Telescope Imaging Spectrograph (STIS)—separates light into a spectrum. Lines in the spectrum tell astronomers what the stars and galaxies are made of, how hot they are, and how fast they are moving.

3 The Near Infrared Camera and Multi-Object Spectrometer (NICMOS)—"sees through" interstellar dust clouds.

4 Faint Object Camera (FOC)—a digital camera that has image intensifiers, which are devices that make very dim images hundreds of times brighter.

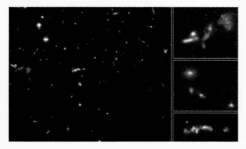

◄ Faint Object Camera view of a distant cluster of galaxies

How does it work?

Light bounces off the telescope's main mirror onto another mirror and then onto scientific instruments behind a hole in the main mirror. Spinning disks called reaction wheels point the telescope at the right part of the sky. Gyroscopes and fine guidance sensors help to keep it pointing in the right direction. Information from the scientific instruments passes to computers, which prepare it to be sent as radio signals from the spacecraft's antennas. Two large solar panels generate electricity, which is stored in batteries.

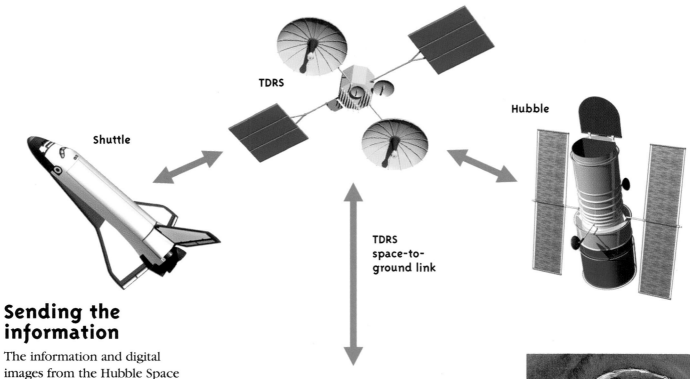

Shuttle

TDRS

Hubble

TDRS space-to-ground link

Sending the information

The information and digital images from the Hubble Space Telescope are sent as radio signals to communications satellites also in orbit around planet Earth. These tracking and data relay satellites (TDRS) pass on the signals to ground-based receiving dishes at the White Sands Ground Terminal in New Mexico. From there, information is passed to the Goddard Space Flight Center in Maryland. Finally, it is sent to the Space Telescope Science Institute at Johns Hopkins University, Maryland, for analysis.

White Sands Ground Terminal

▲ A network of tracking and data relay satellites (TDRS) is used to keep ground stations in touch with important orbiting vehicles, such as the HST and the shuttle.

▲ He gave his name to the HST.

Who was Hubble?

The Hubble Space Telescope is named after Edwin Hubble (1889-1953)—the first person to measure the distance to a galaxy outside our own. Before Hubble's pioneering work, astronomers believed that the fuzzy patches they could see—what we now know are galaxies—were gas clouds inside our own Milky Way Galaxy. They also believed that the Milky Way Galaxy was the entire Universe. Hubble changed our view of the Universe forever, and the telescope that bears his name is doing the same.

Not the first space telescope...

Although the Hubble Space Telescope is the most famous and most successful orbiting observatory, it was not the first. Back in 1966, NASA (the National Aeronautics and Space Administration) launched the first of three Orbiting Astronomical Observatories (OAOs). These were small and very primitive compared to the Hubble Space Telescope, but they were successful: they showed that it was possible to place telescopes in space. Telescopes that are sensitive to X-rays, infrared, ultraviolet, and gamma rays have also been launched into space.

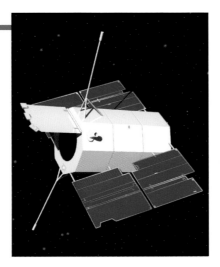

▲ An early space telescope, OAO-3, launched in 1972.

...and not the last!

Designs have been put forward for Next Generation Space Telescope (NGST), planned for launch in 2009. Its 26.2-foot (8-m) mirror will collect 11 times as much light as the Hubble Space Telescope. This will allow it to see objects farther away than ever before. The farther away an object is, the longer light has taken to reach us from it. So the NGST will be able to glimpse stars and galaxies in the very early Universe.

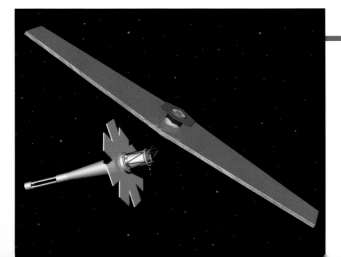

◀ One of the proposed designs for the NGST. The petal-shaped object is the mirror.

THE SOLAR SYSTEM

Long ago, a cloud of gas and dust called a nebula—left over by an exploding dead star—clumped together and began to spin and form a disk. There was a bulge in the middle of the disk that contained most of the material in the clump, and other, smaller lumps formed within the disk. That was how the Solar System began.

The bulge in the center of the early Solar System became the Sun, and the other clumps within the cloud of gas and dust became the nine planets. The leftover material is millions of asteroids, comets, and meteoroids. An asteroid is like a very small planet—some are just a few yards across. Most of the asteroids have orbits between Mars and Jupiter, in what is known as the Asteroid Belt. Comets are made mainly of ice and rocky dust. Meteoroids are much smaller than asteroids and comets—some as small as a speck of dust. All of the objects in the Solar System are held in orbit around the Sun by the force of gravity. Gravity pulls everything together. Without gravity, the planets would travel in straight lines instead of orbits, and there would be no Solar System.

▲ Comet Hayakutake, a bright comet visible from Earth in 1996, with its long tail bright in the night sky

The Oort Cloud

In the outskirts of the Solar System—way beyond the orbits of Neptune and Pluto—is a cloud of rocky, icy nuggets called the Oort Cloud. Astronomers believe that the Oort Cloud is the birthplace of most comets. The Solar System contains thousands of comets, often described as dirty snowballs. Some take only a few months to complete each orbit and others take thousands of years. Comets have orbits that are far from circular, which bring them close to the Sun. There they heat up, releasing ice and dust as a long tail.

▲ Earth has white clouds and a blue atmosphere rich in nitrogen.

What is the Solar System made of?

The cloud of gas and dust from which the Solar System formed was mainly hydrogen and helium gases, and these are still abundant in the Solar System today. Other abundant elements are oxygen, silicon, and nitrogen. Hydrogen and oxygen combine to make water; silicon and oxygen combine to form rocks called silicates. The planets closest to the Sun are made mostly of silicate rocks. Farther out, the gas giants have small rocky cores and thick atmospheres made mainly of hydrogen, helium, and ice. The Earth consists of rock, metal, and gases. Its atmosphere is mainly nitrogen and oxygen.

What is in the Solar System?

The Solar System is made up of:

- 1 star (the Sun)
- 9 planets
- at least 64 moons
- 100,000 minor planets or asteroids more than 1 mile across
- 100 billion comets—"dirty snowballs" several miles across
- Rocky and metallic debris

▼ The *Galileo* probe passed close to asteroid Gaspra (shown here) in 1991.

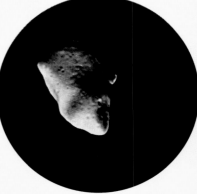

The time taken by these objects to orbit the Sun ranges from 88 days in the case of the innermost planet, Mercury, to more than a million years for the outermost "dirty snowballs."

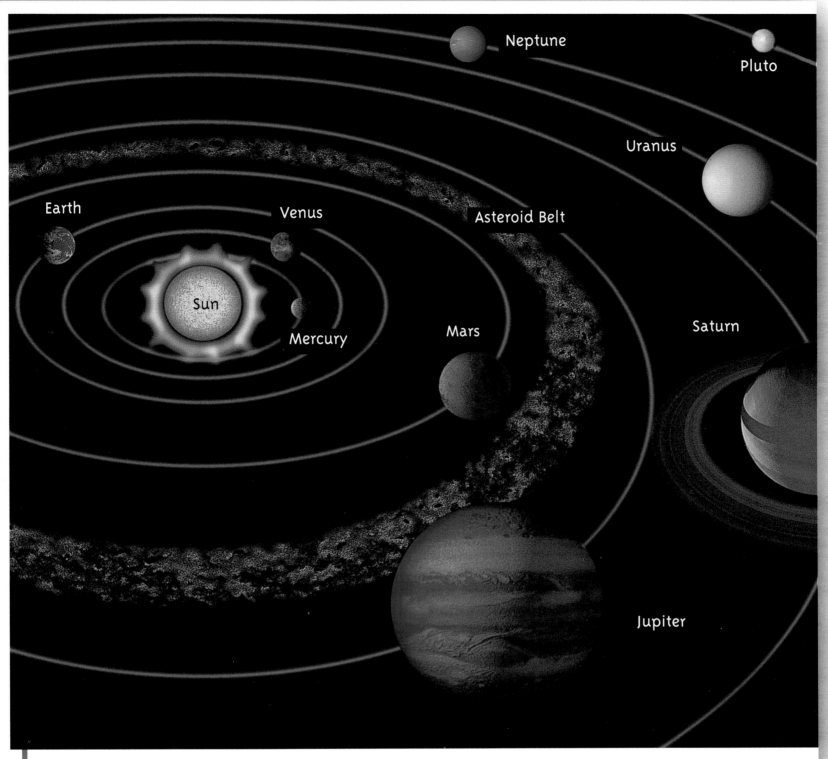

▲ The Sun, the planets, and the Asteroid Belt (not to scale)

Around and around

Earth takes just over 365 days—one year—to complete each orbit of the Sun. Planets closer to the Sun move more quickly and have less distance to travel in each orbit, so they take less time. Most of the planets have natural satellites—moons—orbiting around them, just as the planets themselves orbit the Sun. Looked at from above, each object that orbits the Sun traces out a shape called an ellipse, which is a flattened circle. The orbits of most of the planets are only slightly flattened, while the comets and planet Pluto have orbits that are much more elliptical.

Planet facts

Largest: Jupiter, diameter 88,847 miles (142,985 km)
Smallest: Pluto, diameter 1,442 miles (2,320 km)
Closest approach to Sun: Mercury, 28.5 million miles (46 million km)
Greatest distance from Sun: Pluto, 4.7 billion miles (7.5 billion km)
Longest rotation period: Venus, 243 Earth days
Shortest rotation period: Jupiter, 9 hours 50 minutes
Longest year: Pluto, 249 Earth years
Shortest year: Mercury, 88 Earth days
Hottest average temperature: Venus, 860°F (460°C)
Coldest: Pluto, -380°F (-229°C)
Densest: Earth, 5.52 grams per cubic centimeter
Least dense: Saturn, 0.69 grams per cubic centimeter (Water has a density of 1 gram per cubic centimeter)

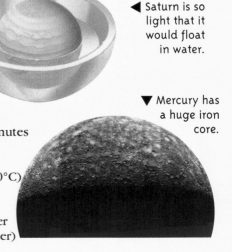

◄ Saturn is so light that it would float in water.

▼ Mercury has a huge iron core.

THE SUN

THE SOLAR SYSTEM

At the center of the Solar System is a glowing ball with a diameter more than 100 times that of Earth. It is our nearest star, the Sun.

Even from our viewpoint 93 million miles (150 million km) away, the Sun is so bright that looking at it directly can harm your eyes. But if the Sun were as far away as even the next nearest star, we would see it as a point of light in a dark sky, just like the stars we see in the night sky. The Sun's surface, at nearly 11,000°F (6,000°C), glows white-hot, sending visible light—and infrared and ultraviolet radiation—in all directions. But deep in the Sun's interior, it is hotter still.

Unlike most matter here on Earth, the Sun is made of plasma. Ordinary matter is made up of countless tiny particles called atoms. Each atom has a central part called a nucleus, surrounded by particles called electrons. At high temperatures, electrons cannot cling to their nuclei, so matter becomes a seething mixture of nuclei and electrons—plasma. Most of the atomic nuclei in the Sun are from atoms of the element hydrogen. The center of the Sun is so hot that hydrogen nuclei are forced to fuse (join together), becoming nuclei of the element helium. This nuclear fusion reaction releases huge amounts of energy, and is the source of the Sun's power.

Radiative zone

Core

Convective zone

▲ A cutaway picture of the Sun. Heat takes hundreds of thousands of years to pass through the radiative zone.

Hot to the core

Solar energy arriving at Earth as sunlight now, left the Sun's surface eight minutes ago. That very same energy was generated in nuclear reactions deep in the Sun's core hundreds of thousands of years ago. At the core, the temperature is about 27 million°F (15m°C). Heat passes from the core to the layer surrounding it, and travels very slowly outward toward the surface through a layer called the radiative zone. Near to the surface is the convective zone, where heat from below bubbles up like boiling water in a pan, making the surface itself a very turbulent place.

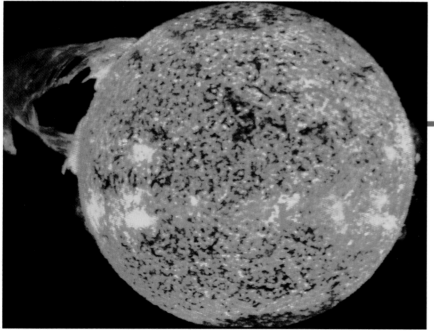

◀ Photographs of the Sun taken through a special filter highlight surface features. This one shows a huge prominence.

The magnetic Sun

The Sun has a very strong magnetic field—which means it acts like a huge magnet. This affects the plasma, which becomes arranged along the lines of magnetic force. The Sun is spinning—it takes about 25 days to rotate once—and this causes the lines of plasma to form twisting loops. These loops of plasma can rise above the surface of the Sun, forming what astronomers call prominences, and eventually snap like stretched rubber bands. When a solar prominence breaks, it throws millions of tons of plasma far out into space.

Mass and energy

The work of physicist Albert Einstein gave the first clues to how the Sun produces energy. Einstein's famous equation $E=mc^2$ describes how mass and energy are related to each other. Mass is a measure of matter. Einstein showed that mass can be converted into energy. As a result of nuclear fusion at its core, the Sun is converting 4.4 million tons (4 million metric tons) of mass per second into an enormous amount of energy.

▲ Albert Einstein (1879–1955)

▲ A photo of the solar disk shows sunspots. Large sunspots are bigger than planet Earth.

The Sun's corona

We see the Sun's photosphere (visible surface) as a very bright circle, which astronomers call the solar disk. Above the photosphere is a thin outer atmosphere that has a temperature of around 3.6 million°F (2 million°C), so hot that it blasts the space around it with powerful X-rays. This outer atmosphere, the solar corona, is normally invisible because the solar disk is so bright. A special instrument called a coronagraph blocks out the photosphere, making the corona visible.

◄ The corona extends 620,000 miles (1,000,000 km) into space.

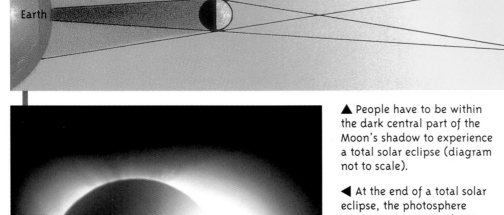

Earth   Moon   Sun

Sunspots and the solar cycle

The Sun's magnetic field drags plasma up and down at the Sun's surface, creating areas that are slightly cooler than the rest of the surface. These areas—called sunspots—appear as darker areas on the Sun's bright disk. The more sunspots present at any one time, the more active is the Sun. The Sun's activity follows a cycle—from high to low and back to high again—over a period of about 11 years. The most recent high point—the solar maximum—was in the year 2000.

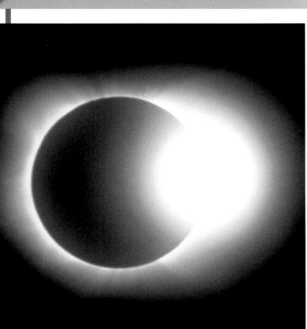

▲ People have to be within the dark central part of the Moon's shadow to experience a total solar eclipse (diagram not to scale).

◄ At the end of a total solar eclipse, the photosphere reappears, causing what is called the diamond ring effect.

Solar eclipse

From Earth, the Sun and the Moon appear to be about the same size—because the Moon is much closer than the Sun. Occasionally, the Moon passes in front of the Sun, so its shadow moves across Earth's surface. This is called a solar eclipse. The center of the Moon's shadow—the umbra—is darkest, and people inside it experience a total solar eclipse. During a total solar eclipse, the daytime sky becomes dark for a few minutes as the Sun disappears completely behind the Moon.

Sun facts

Diameter: 865,000 miles (1,392,000 km)
Mass: 333,000 times greater than Earth's
Average density: 1.41 times denser than water
Rotation period: 25 days 9 hours
Surface gravity: 28 times greater than Earth
Surface temperature: 10,900°F (6,040°C)

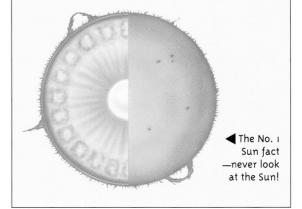

◄ The No. 1 Sun fact —never look at the Sun!

25

MERCURY AND VENUS

The planets Mercury and Venus are known as inferior planets, because they are closer to the Sun than Earth is. For this reason, they are never far from the Sun in the sky, so they can only be seen just before sunrise or just after sunset.

Mercury is a rocky planet with a diameter about one-third that of Earth. Its crust is old and is peppered with craters, many of which are older than the oldest rocks found on Earth. Whichever half of Mercury is turned toward the Sun becomes hot enough to melt lead. The other side of the planet quickly cools to a temperature far below any experienced on Earth. Mercury rotates very slowly, so the planet is always half-hot and half-cold.

Planet Venus is almost exactly the same size as Earth and is similar in many ways: it has volcanoes, an atmosphere, and a rocky surface, for example. However, in many other ways Venus is very different from Earth. The atmosphere on Venus is extremely dense and heavy, and prevents heat from escaping. There is no liquid water, and the atmosphere contains clouds of deadly sulfuric acid, making Venus a hot, dry, and poisonous world.

▼ Thick clouds of acid in Venus's atmosphere hide the surface.

Shrouded in mystery

Venus is the brightest object in the sky apart from the Sun and the Moon. But until about 40 years ago, little was known about it because of the thick clouds that hide the surface from view. The atmosphere of Venus is more than just hard to see through; it is hot and corrosive. Between 1961 and 1983, a series of 16 Soviet spacecraft visited Venus. Most successfully sent back photographs and other information, but none lasted much more than two hours in the hostile conditions inside Venus's atmosphere.

◀ The cratered surface of Mercury makes it look similar to the Moon.

▼ Large craters like this one are common on Mercury's surface.

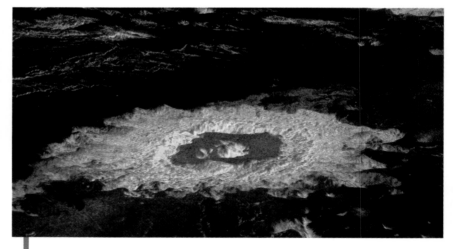

Heavy planet

In 1974, the space probe *Mariner 10* became the only spacecraft so far to visit Mercury. Cameras aboard *Mariner 10* took stunning photographs of the planet's surface and the spacecraft's instruments measured the planet's magnetic field. Mercury has a strong magnetic field because it has a large iron core, more than half as big as the whole planet. This also makes the planet very dense (heavy for its size). A new mission is due to visit the planet again, in 2004.

Mercury's craters

Mercury's surface is covered in craters—the result of impacts by rocks from space called meteoroids. Mercury has only a very thin atmosphere because it is so close to the Sun. So meteoroids reach the surface without slowing down or burning up. Most impacts occurred in the early history of the Solar System, when meteoroids were more common. A large impact disturbs the planet's surface, throwing up perhaps millions of tons of rock and dust—called ejecta. The ejecta often forms characteristic streaks around craters.

The surface of Venus

Venus's surface is always hidden from view by the thick, corrosive clouds of its atmosphere. So we only know what it is like from radar surveys by spacecraft in orbit around the planet, and from brief glimpses of the surface from ground level in photographs taken by the spacecraft that have landed there. The radar surveys reveal that the surface of Venus is dominated by large, flat plains, with gently sloping mountain ranges, volcanoes, and large wide valleys. Most of the surface appears to be very young—perhaps only 500 million years old—indicating that it was renewed by lava spilling out onto it by the many volcanoes. Most of these volcanoes are now extinct (not active).

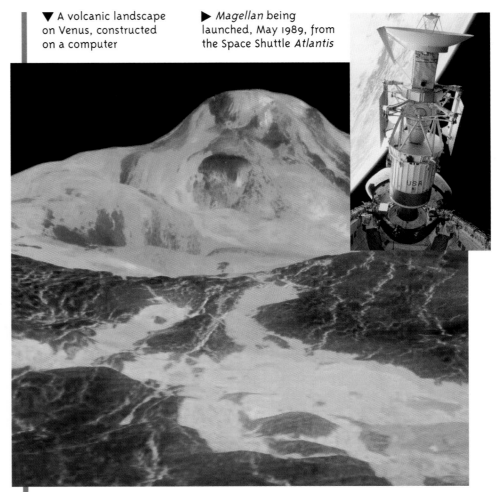

▼ A volcanic landscape on Venus, constructed on a computer

▶ *Magellan* being launched, May 1989, from the Space Shuttle *Atlantis*

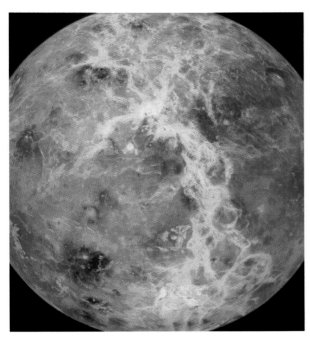

▲ Image put together from space probe *Magellan*'s radar survey. The colors were added by computer.

Lava land

From 1990 to 1994, the American spacecraft *Magellan* orbited Venus, using radar to produce extremely detailed three-dimensional maps of the planet's surface. The maps confirm the idea that Venus's surface features are caused by volcanic activity. Long ago, lava from these now-extinct volcanoes and from cracks in the planet's rocky crust flowed across much of the surface. Lava is molten rock, and when it cools, it solidifies (becomes solid). Lava flows on Venus laid down new rock over ancient craters and explain why the surface is so flat.

The greenhouse effect

Venus's high temperature is due to what scientists call the greenhouse effect. The plants inside a greenhouse absorb the energy of sunlight, which causes them to warm up. The warm plants emit infrared radiation, but the infrared cannot pass through the greenhouse's glass walls. This is why the greenhouse warms up on a sunny day. In the same way, the dense atmosphere of Venus prevents infrared radiation from escaping. The greenhouse effect also occurs on Earth, because of carbon dioxide and other "greenhouse gases" in the atmosphere.

◀ Infrared radiation can't pass through glass, so the greenhouse warms up when the Sun shines.

Sun

Light

Infrared

Mercury and Venus facts

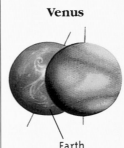

Mercury

Earth

Diameter: 3,032 miles (4,879 km)
Mass: 0.06 as great as Earth's
Density: 5.4 times denser than water
Average distance from Sun: 36 million miles (58m km)
Rotation period: 59 Earth days
Length of year: 88 Earth days
Surface gravity: 0.38 times as great as Earth's
Surface temperature: -274° to 806°F (-170° to 430°C)
Satellites: 0

Venus

Earth

Diameter: 7,521 miles (12,014 km)
Mass: 0.82 times as great as Earth's
Density: 5.2 times denser than water
Average distance from Sun: 67 million miles (108m km)
Rotation period: 243 Earth days
Length of year: 225 Earth days
Surface gravity: 0.90 times as great as Earth's
Surface temperature: 860°F (460°C)
Satellites: 0

THE EARTH

The planet we know most about is the one we can study in great detail without sending spacecraft or gazing through a telescope. Planet Earth is the most interesting and surprising world in the Solar System.

Long ago, people believed that the Earth was flat and that if they traveled far enough, they would fall off the edge. We now know that Earth is a slightly flattened sphere, just like the other planets. We are held on to the Earth by the force of gravity, which pulls us down toward the planet's center. If gravity suddenly switched off, we would float into space. We live at the bottom of a sea of gases called the atmosphere, which is also held on to the planet by gravity. The atmosphere surrounds the planet and helps to keep us alive. Beneath our feet is a solid, rocky crust up to 25 miles (40 km) thick. The crust is divided into sections, or plates, which float around very slowly on molten rock called magma. The magma makes up a layer called the mantle, which surrounds a core made of the metals iron and nickel.

The two objects of the Solar System that are most important for Earth are the Sun and the Moon. The Sun provides energy to warm our planet so that life can thrive, while the gravitational attraction (pulling) between the Earth and the Moon produces tides. The Moon's gravitational attraction is also gradually slowing our planet's rotation.

▲ A chemical called chlorophyll, which is essential in photosynthesis, gives green plants their color.

Our green planet

Earth's atmosphere is composed mainly of the gases oxygen and nitrogen. Oxygen is a very reactive gas, and without some way to replenish it, all of the atmospheric oxygen would soon combine with other chemicals and be lost from the atmosphere. Most of the oxygen in the atmosphere is replenished by a chemical reaction in green plants called photosynthesis. In this process, plants use sunlight, carbon dioxide, and water to make food. They give off oxygen, replenishing oxygen in the atmosphere.

▼ An exaggerated view of the bulging oceans—caused by the gravitational attraction between the Earth and the Moon—that is responsible for the tides.

The rise and fall of the oceans

The daily rising and falling of the tides is caused by the gravitational attraction between the Earth and the Moon, which results in a bulge in the oceans. The gravitational force between two objects depends on the distance between them. The oceans on the side of the Earth nearest to the Moon are pulled the most, the oceans on the other side are pulled the least. As the Earth rotates, the bulges move to different locations.

Slipping and sliding

The Earth's crust is composed of several sections, called plates, which float on the molten magma. The plates are moving at about 2 inches (5 cm) per year. At plate boundaries (the points where any two plates meet), two plates may be moving apart or moving together. Where plates are moving together (convergent boundary), one plate is pushed underneath the other into the mantle, while the other may ride upward, slowly building mountain ranges. Where they move apart (divergent boundary), new crust forms as magma emerges from the mantle. At any plate boundary, disturbances in the crust may cause earthquakes and volcanoes.

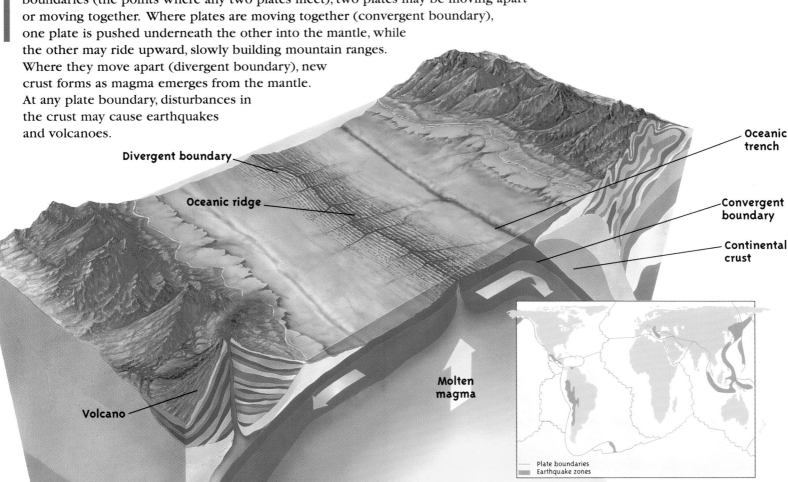

Oceanic trench

Convergent boundary

Continental crust

Divergent boundary

Oceanic ridge

Molten magma

Volcano

Plate boundaries
Earthquake zones

▲ Diagram showing the two different types of boundary (not to scale), with a map showing the plates of the Earth

Hot and cold

The arctic and the antarctic—regions around the North and South Poles—are snow-covered all year, because temperatures there are low. The region around the equator (the middle of the Earth) is always warm. Sunlight arrives at the equator straight-on, so that the Sun appears overhead for people living there. But for people near the poles, the Sun never appears high in the sky, because sunlight arrives at a shallow angle.

Earth facts

Diameter: 7,926 miles (12,756 km)
Mass: 6 sextillion tons (5.5 sextillion tonnes)
Density: 5.5 times denser than water
Average distance from Sun:
  93 million miles (150m km)
Rotation period: 23 hours 56 mins
Length of year: 365 days 5 hours
Surface temperature: -92° to 136°F
  (-69° to 58°C)
Satellites: 1

▼ In four billion years, the Moon will appear to be about half its present size.

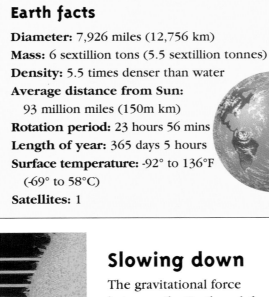

▲ Picture showing sunlight arriving at Earth (not to scale). Notice how the sunlight arrives at a shallow angle at the poles, but straight-on at the equator.

Slowing down

The gravitational force between the Earth and the Moon, which causes the tides, is also slowing down the speed of Earth's rotation. A billion years ago, the length of the day—the time it takes for Earth to rotate once—was about 18 hours, compared to 24 hours today. That same force is also slowing down the Moon as it orbits Earth. The more slowly the Moon travels, the farther from Earth it orbits, and the smaller it appears in our sky.

THE MOON

There are thousands of objects in orbit around Earth —all but one of them are artificial satellites, launched by rockets from Earth. The exception—our only natural satellite—is the second brightest object in our sky: the Moon.

Perhaps the most obvious thing about the Moon is that its shape appears to vary, in a cycle called the lunar phases. Every month, we see the Moon change gradually from completely dark (new moon) to completely lit-up (full moon) and back again, with different amounts of the disk (face) visible in between. The lunar phases occur because the Sun lights up exactly one-half of the Moon's surface at any time, and we see the lit side from different angles as the Moon moves along its orbit around Earth.

So far, the Moon is the only natural object other than Earth that people have visited. People first landed on the Moon in 1969. Until now, only 12 astronauts have walked on the Moon, but it is likely that a permanent base—or even a colony—will be set up there in the future. The greatest obstacles to a lunar base are the lack of air and water on the Moon. However, in 1994, a spacecraft called *Clementine* discovered millions of tons of water ice in a dark crater near the Moon's South Pole. If this discovery is confirmed, it will be much easier to set up a permanent base on the Moon.

▲ On the near side of the Moon, you can see craters and large, dark maria.

The near side

We always see the same side of the Moon, because the Moon takes the same amount of time to rotate once as it takes to orbit Earth. This is a result of the gravitational force between Earth and the Moon, which also puts enormous strain on the Moon's crust. As a result, the near side of the Moon has been cracked many times. Each time, lava (molten rock) spewed onto the surface. The near side of the Moon is dominated by large, flat areas called maria (Latin for "seas," although there is no water), which formed as the lava cooled.

The Moon's phases

As the Moon moves around its orbit—once every 27¼ days— the Sun keeps it half-illuminated. Depending upon where the Moon is in its orbit, different amounts of the lit side are visible from Earth. This results in the Moon's phases, which change over approximately a month. At full moon, the Sun and Moon are on opposite sides of the Earth, so the Moon appears at night. The other phases can be seen at different times of day and night as the Moon waxes (grows from new moon to full moon) and wanes (from full moon back to new moon).

▶ The lunar phases change as the Moon orbits Earth.

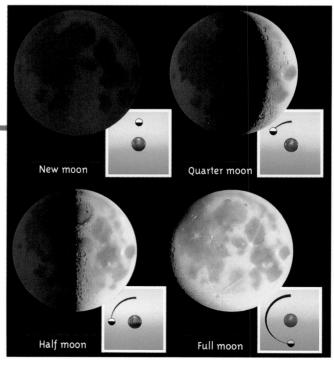

New moon

Quarter moon

Half moon

Full moon

The far side

The half of the Moon that is always turned away from Earth—the far side—was never seen before the Space Age. It was first photographed by a Russian spacecraft called *Luna 3*, in 1959—10 years before people first walked on the Moon. The far side has fewer maria, because the crust there is thicker, making it less likely that molten rock from beneath the crust can emerge onto the surface. There are also many more craters on the far side than on the near side, but space scientists are not sure why.

◀ The heavily cratered far side of the Moon

▼ Typical large crater on the Moon

Moonrock

Astronauts have brought back 900 pounds (400 kg) of moonrock. Moonrock is similar to the rock in Earth's outer layers (the crust and the mantle), but contains no iron (as in the Earth's core). This suggests that the Moon formed from a chunk of Earth knocked off when a huge object hit the Earth early in the history of the Solar System. The Moon's surface is covered with fine, rocky dust produced when rocks from space slam into the lunar surface, forming craters.

Water on the Moon?

In 1994, the spacecraft *Clementine* made a surprising discovery: it found evidence of water ice at the bottom of a deep crater at the Moon's South Pole. In 1998, another spacecraft—*Lunar Prospector*— found more evidence of the ice. To prove that water is present in the crater, space scientists crashed *Lunar Prospector* into the Moon's South Pole. The idea was to throw up some of the ice, making it visible to radio telescopes on Earth. But no ice was detected, so scientists still have no final proof of its existence.

▲ An astronaut collects samples of lunar rock and dust.

Moon facts

Diameter: 2,160 miles (3,476 km)
Mass: 0.012 as great as Earth's
Density: 3.3 times denser than water
Minimum distance from Earth
  (perigee): 221,000 mi. (356,000 km)
Maximum distance from Earth
  (apogee): 253,000 miles (407,000 km)
Rotation period: 27.3 Earth days
Surface temperature: -274° to 230°F (-170° to 110°C)

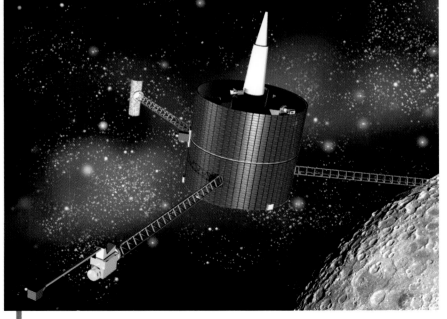

▲ *Lunar Prospector* orbited the Moon and was then crashed into it.

ASTEROIDS AND METEOROIDS

THE SOLAR SYSTEM

Between the orbits of the planets Mars and Jupiter is a belt of orbiting objects called asteroids. Not all asteroids are found here. Some even collide with Earth, heating up as they rub against Earth's atmosphere and producing bright streaks across the sky, called meteors.

Asteroids are much smaller than the planets. The largest, Ceres, is about 590 miles (950 km) in diameter, and only about 250 are more than 60 miles (100 km) across. There are millions of asteroids the size of pebbles. The main belt of asteroids may have been created by a planet that never quite formed early in the Solar System's history or by a planet that formed and then was ripped apart by Jupiter's strong gravity.

Meteors are also called shooting stars, because they look like bright, fast-moving stars streaking across the sky. Most of the objects that cause meteors—called meteoroids—burn up as they pass through Earth's atmosphere. Those that are large enough to reach the ground are called meteorites. Not all meteoroids are asteroids; some are dust particles left in space by comets that pass near to Earth's orbit. When Earth passes through the trail of cometary debris, many meteoroids collide with Earth, causing a meteor shower.

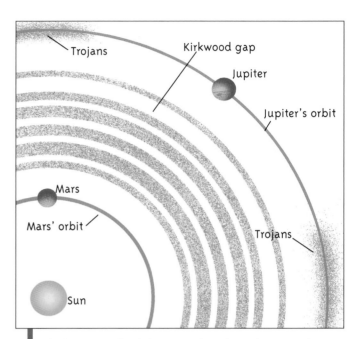

▲ The Asteroid Belt between the orbits of Mars and Jupiter, and the Trojan Asteroids

The Asteroid Belt

About 90 percent of all the asteroids in the Solar System are found in the Asteroid Belt, between the orbits of Mars and Jupiter. Whether the Asteroid Belt represents the remnants of a planet that failed to form, or a planet that formed and was then destroyed, it is likely that Jupiter played a part in the process. Jupiter's gravitational influence has formed gaps in the Asteroid Belt, called Kirkwood Gaps. It also causes asteroids in Jupiter's own orbit to clump together, forming groups known as the Trojan Asteroids.

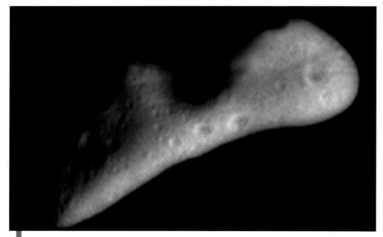

▲ Eros photographed by *NEAR Shoemaker* from 1,100 miles (1,800 km)

Close-up view

Asteroids are so small that no surface details are visible from Earth. The first close-up photographs of them were taken by space probe *Galileo* in 1991. During a more recent project—NEAR (Near Earth Asteroid Rendezvous) —a spacecraft called *NEAR Shoemaker* was sent to explore Eros, an asteroid 21 miles (33 km) long. In 2000, the craft orbited Eros, taking photographs from as near as 3 miles (5 km). In 2001, it landed on Eros's surface.

The meteors in each shower appear to fly from a small part of the sky known as the radiant, so they are named after the constellation where the radiant lies.

Date	Shower	Notes
January 3	Quadrantids	Radiant in Boötes
May 6	Aquarids	Very swift meteors
August 12	Perseids	Many bright meteors

▲ The Barringer Meteor Crater in the Arizona Desert, left by an asteroid impact 50,000 years ago

Craters on Earth

Asteroid impacts were very common early in Earth's history, when asteroids were more numerous. Large asteroids that hit Earth may fall into the oceans, but if they hit land they can scar the landscape with huge craters. Most craters are covered by vegetation or eroded by water. The most famous preserved crater is the Barringer Meteor Crater, formed just 50,000 years ago. Space scientists estimate that it was caused by an asteroid about 150 feet (45 m) across with a mass of hundreds of thousands of tons, traveling at 35,000 miles per hour (60,000 km/h).

Catastrophic impact

A gigantic asteroid hit Earth 65 million years ago, in what is now Mexico, leaving behind a crater 125 miles (200 km) wide. The impact itself would have killed most of the plants and animals across a very wide area. The dust thrown up by the impact would have hung in the air around the world for many years, blocking out sunlight and plunging the planet into a temporary ice age. Some scientists believe that this catastrophic event may have killed the dinosaurs, which became extinct 65 million years ago.

◄ Could the impact of an asteroid have caused the death of the dinosaurs, 65 million years ago?

▲ The study of lunar craters can help predict how asteroids threaten Earth.

▲ In a meteorite from Mars, scientists found what looked like microscopic fossils—signs of ancient life.

▼ Debris left behind in a comet's orbit can cause regular meteor showers.

Shooting stars

Thousands of faint meteors occur every night, as tiny rock fragments strewn around space pass into the upper atmosphere and burn up. Even a meteoroid the size of a grain of sand will produce a bright streak of light. There are also regular showers of meteors lasting several nights, which occur when Earth passes through the debris that comets leave behind. These showers happen at the same time each year, because the debris is always found in the same part of Earth's orbit.

Threats from space

By working out the dates of craters on the Moon, space scientists have been able to calculate that a really big asteroid will hit the Earth on average once every 10 million years. But millions of tons of material fall to Earth from space every year in the form of small meteorites. Most of these are small asteroids or chunks of debris from comets' tails. But 12 meteorites have been identified as coming from Mars—they must have been ejected from the planet after an asteroid slammed into it.

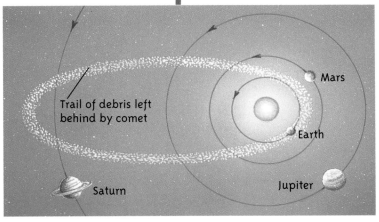

Trail of debris left behind by comet

Mars
Earth
Jupiter
Saturn

MARS

A great deal has been learned about Mars over the past 30 years, thanks to several space probes that have visited the planet. But there are many things that space scientists still want to find out. Perhaps their main question is: "Is there life on Mars?"

Mars is a cold, dry place, with a thin atmosphere and high winds whipping up dust storms across the planet. The Martian landscape has reddish soil and small rocks. There are deep canyons and towering mountains, vast plains, and huge volcanoes. At the North and South Poles are massive ice caps. Unlike those on Earth, these ice caps are made mostly of frozen carbon dioxide, with a little frozen water.

Although there is at most only a small amount of liquid water on Mars today, there is evidence of ancient rivers and seas—improving the chances that life evolved on Mars at some time. Even evidence that life existed long ago would be a mind-blowing discovery. Two probes— *Viking 1* and *Viking 2*—landed on Mars in 1976, looking for signs of life in chemicals in the Martian soil. They found nothing, but future missions are planned, which may settle the question forever.

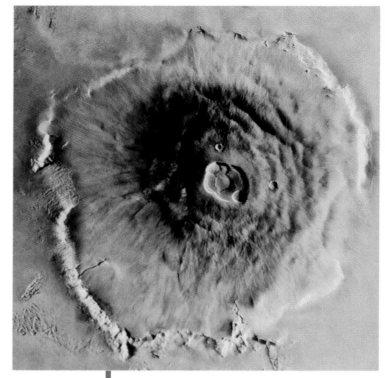

▲ Olympus Mons, a volcano that last erupted at least 25 million years ago

Huge volcano

One of the most famous features of Mars is Olympus Mons—the highest peak in the Solar System. Olympus Mons is an example of a shield volcano, built up over millions of years by lava solidifying as it flows out through a hole in the crust. It stands 15 miles (24 km) high—nearly three times as high as Mount Everest— and has a diameter of more than 300 miles (500 km). Because Earth's crust is always moving, lava can't keep flowing from the same spot to build up a volcano as big as this.

▼ A Martian hurricane about 600 miles (1,000 km) across

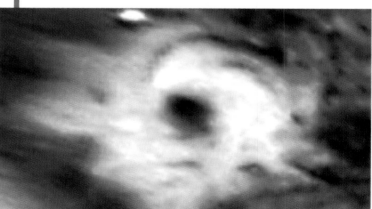

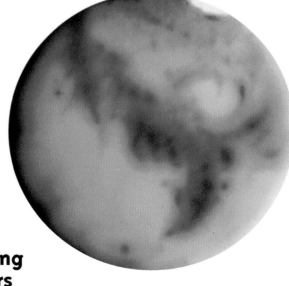

▶ Even from the Hubble Space Telescope, details are hard to see on the Martian surface.

The changing face of Mars

Through telescopes on Earth, only Mars' largest features are visible. The polar ice caps are quite easy to pick out, and astronomers can watch them as they grow and shrink through the changing Martian seasons. Ground-based telescopes can also pick out some cloud formations and follow the shifting shapes of dust storms as they move across the planet. Enormous channels caused by huge cracks in the planet's crust can also be seen.

The Martian climate

The weather on Mars is very changeable. Some days, the sky is cloudless but pinkish with dust carried high into the thin atmosphere by strong winds. Temperatures are at their warmest then—just below freezing. On other days, huge clouds of water ice cover large areas of the planet, and the temperature drops as low as -220°F (-140°C). Huge hurricane-like storms are common. One reason for weather extremes is the variation in Mars' distance from the Sun during its Martian year.

Ancient riverbeds

Stunning close-up photographs of the Martian surface—taken by the space probe *Mars Global Surveyor*, launched in 1997—show many features that seem to have been created by flowing water. It is likely that frozen and liquid water was plentiful in Mars' early history, but that most of it has been lost into space, along with much of the Martian atmosphere. Some space scientists believe most of Mars' water existed underground as ice, flooding the surface when it melted, perhaps after impacts by large meteorites.

▲ A mosiac of images from *Mars Global Surveyor*, showing channels that seem to have been made by flowing water

ALH84001,0

▲ The world's most famous meteorite

Martian fossils?

In 1996, NASA announced that it might have found evidence of life on Mars—in a meteorite called ALH84001, which landed in Antarctica thousands of years ago. It was thrown into space from the Martian surface when an asteroid hit Mars about 16 million years ago. The meteorite contained complex chemicals normally found only in living things and microscopic features that looked like fossils of single-celled organisms. Scientists have found further evidence that the meteorite carried tiny Martian fossils, but no one knows for sure.

The really grand canyon

One of the most impressive geological features on Mars is Valles Marineris, a 2,500-mile (4,000-km) canyon running from east to west along the equator (middle) of the planet. In places, this vast canyon is as deep as 4 miles (7 km) and as wide as 125 miles (200 km). The Grand Canyon in Arizona is only 225 miles (362 km) long, never more than than 1.2 miles (2 km) deep, and never wider than 20 miles (30 km). The Valles Marineris was formed by a rifting (separation) of Mars' crust, caused by a welling up of the magma (molten rock) beneath the surface. The magma probably welled up through a weak spot in the crust—and the weak spot probably developed from stress in the crust when it first solidified.

▼ Part of the huge Valles Marineris canyon, shaped through erosion by wind and perhaps by water

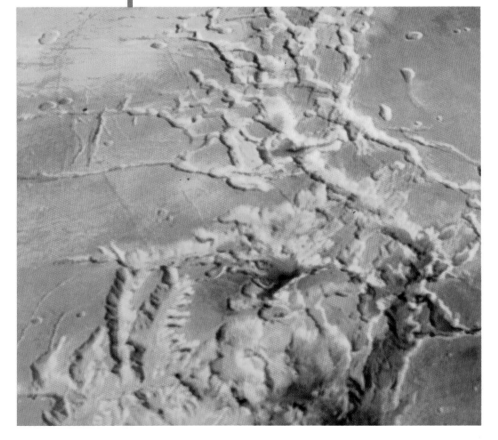

Mars facts

Earth

Diameter: 4,222 mi. (6,794 km)
Mass: 0.107 times greater than Earth's
Density: 3.9 times denser than water
Average distance from Sun: 142 million miles (228m km)
Rotation period: 24 hours 37 minutes
Length of year: 687 Earth days
Surface gravity: 0.38 as great as Earth's
Surface temperature: -220° to 32°F (-140°C to 0°C)
Satellites: 2 (Phobos and Deimos)

JUPITER

THE SOLAR SYSTEM

Imagine trying to land on Jupiter. Approaching what looks like the surface of the planet, you go down through a thin layer of icy clouds. The clouds become thicker, the temperature rises, and the clouds gradually change into a strange, very thick and extremely hot liquid. Finally, after traveling 44,000 miles (70,000 km), you hit a solid surface.

Of the Solar System's gas giant planets, Jupiter is nearest to the Sun. While Earth, Venus, and Mars are mostly rock surrounded by a thin atmosphere, Jupiter and the other gas giants are mainly atmosphere surrounding a small, rocky core. Although Jupiter has a diameter more than 11 times the diameter of Earth, the rocky core is not much bigger than the whole of Earth. In 1995, the *Galileo* atmospheric probe made the journey into Jupiter's atmosphere. As it fell, the probe measured temperature and pressure, and analyzed the chemical composition of the atmosphere. After an hour, when the probe was about 90 miles (150 km) below the clouds, it stopped sending signals, but it continued its long fall toward Jupiter's core. Several other probes have visited Jupiter and investigated the planet and its many moons, the four largest of which were discovered by Galileo in 1610.

▲ Swirling bands of cloud can be seen on the surface of Jupiter, which is the largest planet in the Solar System.

Gas giant

From Earth, planet Jupiter is visible with the naked eye as a bright yellowish point of light. Through binoculars or a small telescope, the four Galilean satellites (discovered by Galileo) become visible, and through a medium-sized telescope, an observer can pick out surface features, such as a huge storm called the Great Red Spot. Jupiter rotates very rapidly—it makes a complete turn in less than 10 hours. This speedy rotation causes the clouds to form several swirling bands.

▶ An artist's impression of the clouds at Jupiter's "surface"

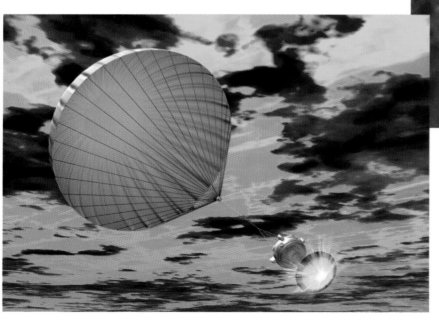

▲ The *Galileo* probe used a parachute to descend into Jupiter's atmosphere.

Heavy clouds

There is no real surface on Jupiter—the atmosphere just thins out with altitude (height). So astronomers define the surface of the planet as the distance from the center of the planet where the atmospheric pressure is the same as the atmospheric pressure at the surface of Earth. The *Galileo* atmospheric probe, deployed in December 1995, analyzed the cloud tops at that level. They were composed mostly of frozen ammonia, but also included water ice and droplets of liquid water, along with a cocktail of other chemicals.

Jupiter's Galilean satellites

- **Io** takes 42 hours to revolve around Jupiter. Its diameter is 2,256 miles (3,630 km)—about the same as our Moon. See below.
- **Europa** takes 3½ days to revolve around Jupiter. It has a diameter of 1,939 miles (3,120 km). It is a rocky moon covered with a thin layer of ice.
- **Callisto** has a diameter of 2,986 miles (4,806 km) and takes nearly 17 days to orbit Jupiter. It is rocky and has a heavily cratered surface.
- **Ganymede** is the largest satellite in the Solar System, with a diameter of 3,273 miles (5,268 km). It probably has a small core of molten iron with a rocky mantle covered by a layer of ice.

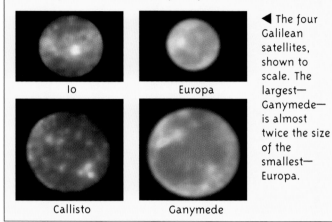

Io   Europa

Callisto   Ganymede

◀ The four Galilean satellites, shown to scale. The largest—Ganymede—is almost twice the size of the smallest—Europa.

▲ The Great Red Spot and another storm, a white oval storm

The Great Red Spot

Heat produced deep in the atmosphere warms the clouds, making them rise. This produces the bands that stretch around the planet and leads to the formation of large, spinning storm systems like hurricanes on Earth. The largest and longest-lived of these is called the Great Red Spot, but Jupiter also has many large white oval storms. The Great Red Spot is the largest storm system in the Solar System—its diameter is more than twice that of Earth. It is also at least 300 years old—it was first observed in the 1600s.

Volcanic Io

When the *Voyager 1* space probe flew past Jupiter in 1979, space scientists were hoping to find out how old Io is by counting the craters on its surface. However, few craters were found, indicating that the surface of Io is very young. It is continually renewed by lava, erupting from volcanoes. *Voyager* sent back stunning photos of active volcanoes throwing lava up to a height of 186 miles (300 km). The source of Io's heat is Jupiter's strong gravitational influence, which bends and stretches its moon.

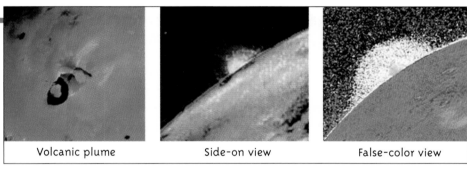

Volcanic plume   Side-on view   False-color view

▲ Photographs of Io's volcanoes taken by *Voyager 1*

Almost a star

Jupiter has so much mass that gravity pulls the gas tightly towards the center, increasing the temperature and pressure to unimaginably high levels. For this reason, Jupiter gives out more heat than it receives from the Sun. If it were about 10 times the size it is, the temperature at the core would be hot enough for nuclear fusion reactions to take place, and Jupiter would be a type of dim star, called a brown dwarf. If it were about 60 times the size, it would be a star just like the Sun.

Small rocky core surrounded by metallic hydrogen

Thick gaseous atmosphere

◀ The solid core of Jupiter is surrounded by a strange liquid called metallic hydrogen.

Liquid mantle

Jupiter facts

Earth

Diameter: 88,846 miles (142,984 km)

Mass: 318 times greater than Earth's

Density: 1.3 times denser than water

Average distance from Sun: 483 million miles (778m km)

Rotation period: 9 hours 50 minutes at equator

Length of year: 11 years 315 days

Surface gravity: 2.5 times as great as Earth's

Surface temperature: -256°F (-160°C)

Satellites: at least 16

SATURN

The most stunning planet of the Solar System is Saturn. Its beautiful rings are visible even with a small telescope. It is the furthest of the five planets known to the ancients—and the least bright planet visible to the naked eye.

The first person to see Saturn's rings was the 17th-century Italian astronomer Galileo. In 1610, he saw the rings through his small homemade telescope and wrote that Saturn has what look like ears. Later in the same century, other astronomers used better telescopes to look at Saturn and identified the ears as rings around the planet. All of the gas giant planets have ring systems, but Saturn's are by far the biggest. The icy chunks of which the rings are made reflect a good deal of the sunlight that falls on them, making them the brightest, too. In other ways, Saturn is very similar to Jupiter. It has a small, very hot rocky core, surrounded by liquid "metallic" hydrogen and then atmosphere gradually thinning all the way out into space. Saturn's cloud tops are composed mostly of ammonia, water ice, hydrogen, and helium. Beyond the cloud tops—in orbit around the huge planet—are Saturn's moons. There are at least 18 moons and probably 24—the largest collection of moons for any planet in the Solar System.

▲ An artist's impression of the rings of Saturn seen from the planet's cloud tops

▲ Saturn is tilted in its orbit. The best time to see the rings is when the planet's tilt is in the direction of Earth.

Views of the rings

Like Earth, Saturn orbits the Sun like a tilted spinning top. As Saturn travels around its orbit, we see it from different directions, so we see the rings at different angles. The best times for viewing Saturn are when the planet's tilt is pointing toward us—at these times, we see a large area of the rings. Sometimes, we see the planet from the side, so that we see the rings completely edge-on—at these times, the rings appear to disappear, because they are very thin.

Saturn's atmosphere

The rapid rotation of Saturn causes bands to appear in its gaseous atmosphere, just like on Jupiter. However, Saturn's bands are not as well defined as Jupiter's. In fact, Saturn's atmosphere has very few noticeable features. This is due to the layer of haze normally present above the cloud tops. Even close-up photographs taken by visiting space probes show Saturn's atmosphere to be quite featureless, although every 30 years or so, a huge white oval storm develops near the planet's equator, a storm about the same diameter as Earth.

◀ Saturn is a huge, hazy ball of gas. Notice the shadow of the planet cast across the rings and the white oval storm.

Flat and wide

Saturn's rings are huge flat disks as much as 155,000 miles (250,000 km) in diameter and only about half a mile (1 km) thick. If you made a scale model where the rings were as thin as a sheet of cardboard, they would have a diameter of nearly 400 feet (122 m). The rings are made of chunks of water ice or rock with an icy coating which revolve around Saturn like billions of tiny moons. The largest chunks in the rings are about 15 feet (5 m) in diameter.

▲ False color, close-up image of the rings taken by *Voyager 2*. Each ring is made of many smaller ringlets.

▲ Saturn's moons keep the lumps of ice and rock of the rings together.

Shepherd moons

Many of Saturn's small moons orbit in the gaps between the rings. The gravitational force between these moons and the chunks of ice and rock in the rings helps to keep the rings tidy. If any particles in the rings stray out of line as they orbit Saturn, the gravitational force nudges them back again, a little like shepherds keeping their flocks of sheep together. Astronomers actually call these moons "shepherding satellites." Shepherding works most effectively when two moons have similar orbits.

Naming the moons

Saturn's moons are named after characters from Greek mythology—the Titans. The Titans were sons and daughters of Gaia (the earth) and Uranus (the sky). The naming system was suggested by John Herschel in 1847. John's father was William Herschel, who discovered two of Saturn's moons, Mimas and Enceladus (as well as the planet Uranus). These are strange moons, made mostly of water ice, with only a little rock. Mimas has a huge crater on its surface, while Enceladus is shinier than any other planet or moon in the Solar System.

Life on Titan?

The largest of Saturn's moons is Titan. It has a dense atmosphere—unusually for a moon—of nitrogen and methane gas. The methane in the upper atmosphere breaks down to form a thick smog, obscuring the surface. Other interesting gases are present, including ethane, carbon dioxide, and water. This unusual mixture of chemicals has led astronomers to suggest that some form of life may exist in oceans of liquid methane on the surface of Titan. In 2005, the space probe *Huygens* will penetrate Titan's atmosphere to take photographs and analyze whatever it finds on the surface.

▼ Artist's impression of Saturn as seen from the surface of Titan

▲ Titan is shrouded by a thick layer of smog.

▲ Mimas has a huge crater, called Herschel.

▲ Enceladus' shiny surface is covered with fresh ice.

Saturn facts

Diameter: 74,897 miles (120,536 km)
Mass: 95 times greater than Earth's
Density: 0.7 times denser than water
Average distance from Sun: 888 million miles (1.429 billion km)
Rotation period: 10 hours 39 minutes at equator
Length of year: 29 years 167 days
Surface gravity: 0.9 times as great as Earth's
Surface temperature: -310°F (-190°C)
Satellites: At least 18

Earth

URANUS AND NEPTUNE

The planets Uranus and Neptune have a good deal in common. They are blue, featureless gas giants of about the same size, they both have systems of rings, and both have been visited by only one spacecraft. *Voyager 2* **flew past Uranus in 1986 and past Neptune in 1989.**

Uranus was the first planet to be discovered since ancient times. It is not quite visible to the naked eye, so could not have been spotted before the invention of the telescope in the early 1600s. Uranus was first spotted in 1690, but at that time it was thought to be a star. It was not until 1781 that it was recognized as a planet, by German-born English astronomer William Herschel. Neptune was discovered more than 60 years later, in 1846, using new mathematics as well as telescopes. Astronomers realized that another large object was present in the outer Solar System, because the orbit that they had predicted for Uranus was different from the one they observed. They worked out where the mystery planet might be, and when astronomers looked for it with their telescopes in 1846, the new planet was found in that part of the sky.

Despite the fact that both Uranus and Neptune were discovered a long time ago, little was known about the planets until *Voyager 2* sped past them.

▲ *Voyager 2* traveling past Uranus. You can also see Puck, a moon discovered by *Voyager 2*.

Lone visitor

After visiting Jupiter and Saturn, *Voyager 2* passed Uranus, approaching as close as 50,000 miles (80,000 km) above the cloud tops—a quarter the distance between Earth and the Moon. It ventured even closer to Neptune, flying only 3,000 miles (5,000 km) above that planet's north pole. *Voyager 2* sent back thousands of intriguing images and information from its many scientific instruments, including measurements of the planets' strong magnetic fields.

The discovery of Uranus

William Herschel's early career was in music, but he became interested in the study of astronomy and started to make his own telescopes. In an attempt to produce a catalog of all the objects he could observe through his telescopes, he carried out three detailed surveys of the sky. It was during the third survey that he noticed a slightly fuzzy object, which had moved by the time he looked at it again four days later. Herschel thought it might be a comet, but what he had discovered was a new planet—Uranus.

◄ One of Herschel's early telescopes

◄ William Herschel (1738–1822) was given an income by King George III, so that he could concentrate on astronomy.

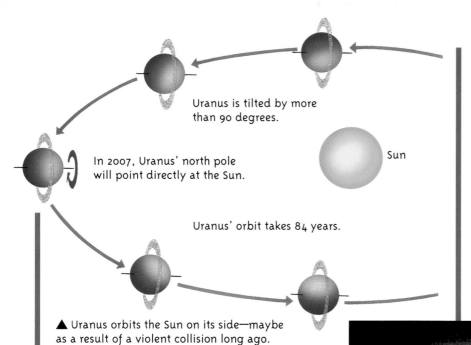

Uranus is tilted by more than 90 degrees.

In 2007, Uranus' north pole will point directly at the Sun.

Sun

Uranus' orbit takes 84 years.

▲ Uranus orbits the Sun on its side—maybe as a result of a violent collision long ago.

Sideways on

All the planets—including Earth—are tilted slightly, so their north and south poles point toward and away from the Sun at different points around their orbits. That is why we have seasons on Earth. Uranus' seasons are very extreme, because the planet is tilted right over onto its side. At different times during its 84-year orbit, both the north pole and the south pole point directly at the Sun. In 2007, Uranus will be side-on to the Sun, so that the Sun will be directly above the planet's equator.

Cold and blue

The temperature at the cloud tops of Uranus is about -184°F (-120° C), and deeper in the atmosphere it gets to -328°F (-200° C). Neptune is slightly colder than Uranus. Fierce winds blow in the atmospheres of both planets. Their blue color comes from methane in the upper atmosphere. Underneath it is a mantle composed mainly of hydrogen, helium, water ice, and ammonia. There may be interesting features below the upper atmosphere, but they are hidden from view.

▶ Neptune's winds are the fastest in the Solar System, raging at up to 1,250 mph (2,000 km/h). The dark spots are huge storms.

◀ Uranus has very few visible surface details, but the planet's atmosphere is known to be very active, with strong winds and huge streams of rising and falling clouds.

Ring systems

The rings around Uranus were discovered by accident, while astronomers were watching the planet move in front of a star. The star flickered on and off before the planet reached it, suggesting the rings' existence. In the 1980s, the same sort of observation alerted astronomers to the existence of rings around Neptune. The findings of *Voyager 2* helped prove the rings were real.

▲ An image from *Voyager 2* of two of Neptune's rings

Twenty-eight moons

Uranus has at least 20 moons, including a very unusual one called Miranda. There are hardly any craters on the surface of Miranda, suggesting it is a very new surface. That is usually only true of planets or moons with volcanoes, where lava floods out to make a new surface. But Miranda has no volcanoes. One theory to explain its appearance is that it broke into pieces and re-formed. Neptune has eight moons. One, Triton, is much larger than the others. It is the coldest place in the Solar System.

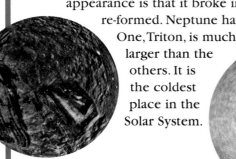

▲ Miranda remains a mystery.

▶ Triton, a very cold place

Uranus and Neptune facts

Uranus
Earth

Diameter: 31,763 miles (51,118 km)
Mass: 14.5 times greater than Earth's
Density: 1.3 times denser than water
Average distance from Sun: 1.784 billion miles (2.871 billion km)
Rotation period: 17 hours 14 minutes
Length of year: 84 Earth years
Surface gravity: 0.8 times as great as Earth's
Surface temperature: -355°F (-215°C)
Satellites: 20

Neptune
Earth

Diameter: 30,803 miles (49,572 km)
Mass: 17.1 times greater than Earth's
Density: 1.6 times denser than water
Average distance from Sun: 2.799 billion miles (4.504 billion km)
Rotation period: 16 hours 7 minutes
Length of year: 165 Earth years
Surface gravity: 1.1 times as great as Earth's
Surface temperature: -373°F (-225°C)
Satellites: 8

41

PLUTO AND BEYOND

The ninth and, as far as we know, the most distant planet from the Sun is a small rocky object called Pluto. Since its discovery in 1930, the few details astronomers have uncovered about Pluto show that it is very different from the other planets. In fact, some astronomers do not consider Pluto a planet at all.

All the planets except Pluto orbit the Sun as if they were on the same invisible, flat racetrack —the ecliptic plane. Pluto's orbit is more like a comet's, because it is tilted, taking the planet far above and below the ecliptic plane. Also like a comet, there is a huge difference between the points of Pluto's orbit closest and farthest from the Sun. In fact, for 20 years of its 248-year orbit, it is closer to the Sun than Neptune is. No other planet crosses another's path like this.

Pluto has a large moon, Charon, more than half its size. And in the past 10 years, many other distant objects—some nearly as big as Pluto—have been discovered. This collection of mysterious icy worlds is called the Kuiper Belt. No spacecraft has yet visited Pluto and Charon or the Kuiper Belt, which are so far away that even the best photographs show only the largest details. Future space missions—perhaps arriving at Pluto by 2020—will have much to teach us about the outer reaches of the Solar System.

An icy world

Space scientists have been able to work out the diameters of Pluto and Charon accurately, because the pair often cross in front of each other. From measurements made with instruments called spectrometers, along with estimates of Pluto's density, we can make a guess about what Pluto is made of. It seems to be mainly frozen methane mixed with rock and frozen nitrogen. Some of the methane vaporizes (becomes a gas) during the planet's closest approach to the Sun, forming a thin methane atmosphere.

▲ Artist's impression of a view of Pluto's moon, Charon, from the surface of Pluto

▼ This photograph of Pluto and Charon taken by the Hubble Space Telescope is one of the clearest obtained so far.

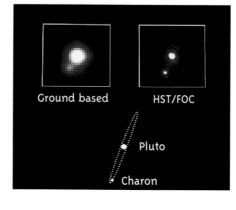

Ground based   HST/FOC

Pluto

Charon

Blurred view

Pluto and Charon are so far away that telescopes cannot view them in any detail. Telescopes on Earth, peering through our atmosphere, see no more than hazy blobs. The Hubble Space Telescope provides astronomers with their clearest views of space, and has produced the best images yet of these two distant worlds. These images show Pluto and Charon in sharp focus, picking them out as two separate objects. But even the best Hubble Space Telescope photographs show only fuzzy dark and light areas.

Hunting for distant worlds

The best way to find dim and distant objects in our Solar System is to take two or more photographs of the same part of the sky several days apart. Any objects in the Solar System move across the fixed background of stars and can be picked out by comparing the photographs. A device called a blink comparitor illuminates first one photograph and then the other. The search for Pluto began in 1905, and American astronomer Clyde Tombaugh eventually found the planet by comparing photographs he took on January 23rd and 29th, 1930. The photographs were captured through a refracting telescope at the Lowell Observatory in Arizona.

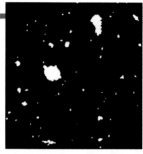

▶ By comparing two images of the same part of the sky, astronomer Clyde Tombaugh was able to pinpoint Pluto, a dim and distant Solar System object moving relative to the stars.

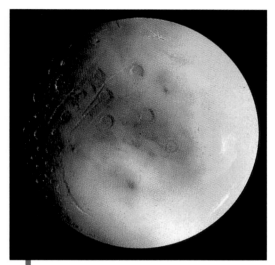

▲ Artist's impression of what a space probe might see when it visits Pluto

Mysterious planet

Pluto seems to be very similar to Neptune's moon Triton—both are made largely of methane and nitrogen ice mixed with rock. Before the discovery of Charon in 1978, some astronomers suggested that Pluto might once have been a moon of Neptune, which had been knocked out of its orbit long ago. But the discovery of objects with orbits similar to Pluto's in the Kuiper Belt has led many astronomers to believe that Pluto is more like an asteroid than a planet.

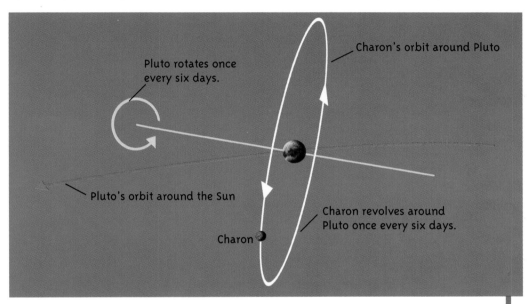

Pluto rotates once every six days.

Charon's orbit around Pluto

Pluto's orbit around the Sun

Charon revolves around Pluto once every six days.

Charon

▲ Charon moves over and under Pluto, completing each orbit in six days—the same amount of time it takes for Pluto to rotate.

Pluto facts

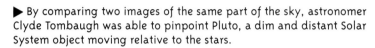

Diameter: 1,442 miles (2,320 km)
Mass: 0.002 as great as Earth's
Density: 2.0 times denser than water
Average distance from Sun: 3.674 billion miles (5.914 billion km)
Rotation period: 6 days 9 hours
Length of year: 248 Earth years
Surface gravity: 0.04 times as great as Earth's
Surface temperature: -382°F (-230°C)
Satellites: 1

Earth

Moon dance

Pluto's orbit around the Sun is unusual, but Charon's orbit around Pluto is stranger still. Most moons revolve around their planets more or less in line with the ecliptic plane, but Charon revolves over and under Pluto. The planet and its moon are more similar in size than any other planet and its moon. Over millions of years, gravitational forces between Pluto and Charon have synchronized (made the same) the rotation of Pluto and the time it takes for Charon to orbit it. This means they always keep the same face turned toward each other. Standing on one side of Pluto, you would always see Charon hanging motionless in the sky, while on the other side, you would never see it.

The Kuiper Belt

During the 1990s, more than 80 icy objects were discovered with orbits similar to Pluto's. They probably formed from material left over after the formation of the Solar System, and are called Plutinos, or simply Kuiper Belt objects. Little is known about them, but they seem to be icy worlds like Pluto and Charon. Many astronomers believe that when Kuiper Belt objects come close to each other, they may get nudged into different orbits and become comets.

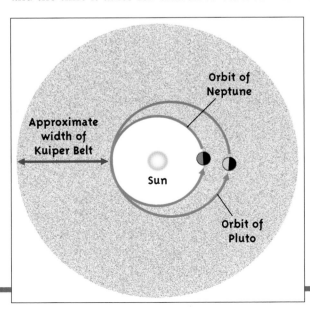

Approximate width of Kuiper Belt

Orbit of Neptune

Sun

Orbit of Pluto

◀ The Kuiper Belt is like the Asteroid Belt, but the objects found there are much colder. It extends from the orbit of Neptune to the outer reaches of the Solar System and may be the source of some comets.

COMETS

Throughout history, people have reported seeing fuzzy objects with long tails that move across the night sky for a few weeks, then fade away. These objects are comets, and there are many more of them in the Solar System than the ones we see in the sky.

It was Edmund Halley (1656-1742) who demonstrated that comets orbit the Sun. This was the first major breakthrough. The second happened within living memory when it was realized that comets are not unusual—it is just that fewer than a million millionth of all the comets that exist in the Solar System have ever been seen.

Comets were once thought to be bad omens—signs that terrible things were about to happen. We now know this is not true; these white, fuzzy objects that sometimes grace our skies are simply huge clouds of dust and ice orbiting the Sun, lit by sunlight. At the nucleus of a comet is a "dirty snowball" several miles in diameter. When the comet passes near the Sun, a cloud of dust and gas—the coma—is released. Comets revolve around the Sun in very irregular orbits; unlike the planets, their closest distance to the Sun is very different from their farthest distance. Comets are made of material left over from the formation of the Solar System, and they may hold many clues to its history.

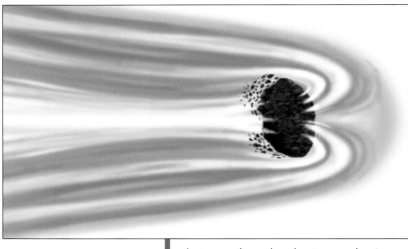

▲ A comet's nucleus heats up, releasing gas and dust as it nears the Sun.

What is a comet?

Comets are only visible because sunlight reflects off them. By analyzing the reflected light, space scientists have found out what comets are made of. The nucleus of a comet consists of rocky dust and ice—water ice, dry ice (frozen carbon dioxide), and frozen methane. Near the Sun, the nucleus warms up and the ices vaporize, releasing dust and gas into space. The coma can be as much as 60,000 miles (100,000 km) in diameter, and the tail can stretch for millions of miles.

▲ Comet science pioneer Edmund Halley

Halley's Comet

Most comets can be seen time and time again because they orbit the Sun. One of the most famous is Halley's Comet, which is seen every 76 years. Edmund Halley, a friend of Isaac Newton, used Newton's theory of gravitation to work out the orbits of 24 comets. He realized some comets appear more than once, and in 1705, he predicted that a comet seen in 1682 would reappear in 1758. Halley died before 1758, but when the comet did reappear, it was named for him.

▲ A comet crossing the ecliptic plane. Its tail always points away from the Sun.

Cometary orbits

Most astronomers believe that far beyond the orbits of Neptune and Pluto, surrounding the Solar System, is the birthplace of most comets, called the Oort Cloud. Gravitational forces between objects there can nudge them in the direction of the Sun. As they move toward the Sun, some go into orbit around it, taking anywhere from a few months to thousands of years for each revolution.

One head, two tails

Bright comets appear to have two tails that point in slightly different directions. In fact, this is true of all comets. The tails are made of the two different types of material released from a comet's nucleus: gas and dust. The solar wind—a stream of high-speed particles from the Sun—pushes both types of material away from the Sun. The gas is made of individual atoms and molecules, and forms a straight tail. The dust particles are too heavy to be pushed into a straight line, so they form a curved tail as the comet sweeps around its orbit.

◀ From Earth, most comets appear as small, misty smudges in the sky. Really bright ones are rare, but they are a beautiful sight—some are even visible during the day.

Collision course

Like asteroids, comets sometimes crash into the Earth and the other planets. Luckily, this happens less often than it did in the early Solar System. However, in 1994, astronomers were given a rare treat: they observed a comet striking the planet Jupiter. Astronomers at hundreds of observatories around the world—and observers using the Hubble Space Telescope—watched excitedly as Jupiter's gravitational effect ripped the comet apart and pulled the pieces into its atmosphere one by one over a period of seven days.

▶ Comet Shoemaker-Levy 9, discovered in 1993, left these "bruises" as its fragments fell into Jupiter's atmosphere in July 1994. The photo was taken by the Hubble Space Telescope.

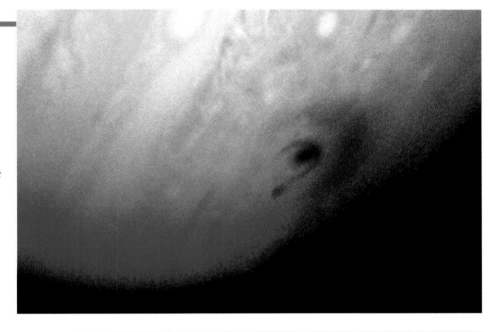

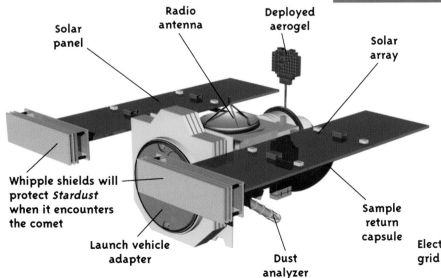

Solar panel — Radio antenna — Deployed aerogel — Solar array — **Whipple shields will protect *Stardust* when it encounters the comet** — Launch vehicle adapter — Dust analyzer — Sample return capsule

▲ Samples from Comet Wild 2 will be captured in an unusual material called an aerogel. The main part of the spacecraft is about the size of an office desk.

▶ *Stardust* can capture and analyze some dust while the spacecraft is still in space. Static electricity will be used to make tiny particles stick to the dust analyzer.

Sweeping up

Comets are like chunks of ancient Solar System history, because unlike the planets they have remained unchanged since the birth of the Solar System about 4.6 billion years ago. In 1999, NASA launched a spacecraft called *Stardust*, which is currently on course for a comet called Wild 2. It should encounter the comet in 2004, passing through the coma about 100 miles (150 km) from the nucleus. During its encounter, *Stardust* will collect samples of the dust and gas from the comet's coma and return them to Earth for analysis in 2006.

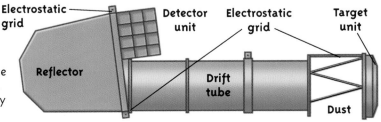

Electrostatic grid — Detector unit — Electrostatic grid — Target unit — Reflector — Drift tube — Dust

DEEP SPACE

The stars that we see in the night sky are all much farther away than the Sun. Light from the Sun takes about eight minutes to reach us, while light from the next nearest star takes more than four years. But even the individual stars that we see are nearby compared to the enormous distances between the galaxies in deep space.

Not until the 1830s did astronomers first begin to work out the distances to the stars. Later that century, they began to discover what stars are made of, and in the 20th century they finally solved the mystery of how stars shine. Today, we have a detailed knowledge about how stars are born, how they develop, and how they die. Modern telescopes allow astronomers to see objects so far away that the radiation we receive from them has taken 12 billion years to reach us. The most distant objects viewed so far are called quasars—energetic galaxies at the edge of the observable Universe. Their light has taken so long to reach us that they provide vital clues to the mystery of what happened at the beginning of time and space.

▲ Our galaxy—a huge collection of stars. The arms of the spiral gradually wind around the central bulge as the galaxy rotates.

Our neighborhood

The Sun is a tiny dot in one of the arms of a vast spiral collection of stars—the Milky Way Galaxy. There are about 200 billion stars in our galaxy, most of them separated by distances that would take hundreds of years to reach using today's fastest spacecraft. If you are planning to take a journey to deep space, the Milky Way Galaxy is just the first step. There are at least 100 billion other galaxies just as big as this, separated by even greater distances.

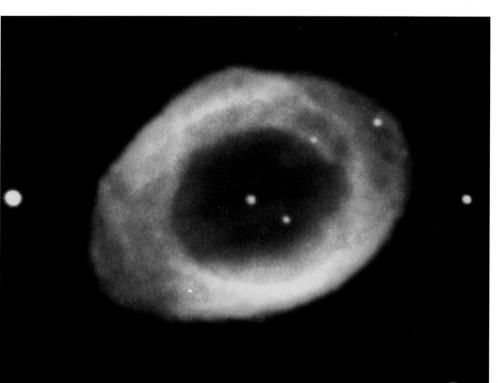

Clouds in space

Stars are not living things, but astronomers often use words like "birth," "death," and "life cycles" when they talk about them. New stars are born all the time, in vast clumps of gas and dust, formed from the interstellar medium—an extremely thin material that fills the space in galaxies. When newborn stars begin to shine, they illuminate these clumps of gas and dust, called nebulas, causing them to glow like huge multicolored clouds. Dying stars add to the interstellar medium by throwing off their outer layers, putting on huge cosmic firework displays. The clouds of dust and gas that they throw out are also called nebulas. A common type is called a planetary nebula because through a small telescope it looks like a planet.

◄ The Ring Nebula is a circle of gas and dust thrown off by a dying star in our galaxy. You can see the star at the center of the ring.

Distances to some stars

Name	Constellation	Distance (in light-years)
● Alpha Centauri	Centaurus (the Centaur)	4.3
● Sirius	Canis Major (the Great Dog)	8.6
● Procyon	Canis Minor (the Small Dog)	11.4
● Vega	Lyra (the Lyre)	25.0
● Arcturus	Boötes (the Herdsman)	34.5
● Capella	Auriga (the Charioteer)	41.9
● Regulus	Leo (the Lion)	69.5
● Canopus	Carina (the Keel)	74 approx.
● Rigel	Orion (the Hunter)	1,400 approx.
● Deneb	Cygnus (the Swan)	1,500 approx.

How far are the stars?

German astronomer Friedrich Bessel was the first person to accurately measure the distance to a star—using an effect called parallax—in 1836. If you face a wall and hold your finger about 20 inches (50 cm) in front of your face, you can see how this works. With one eye closed, look at your finger and move your head from side to side. You will see your finger appear to move. The closer your finger is to your face, the more you see it move. Bessel noted the position of the star in the sky at two different times, six months apart.

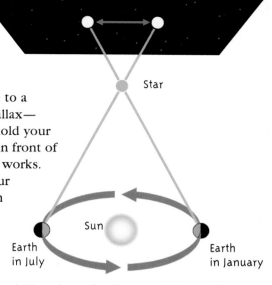

▲ If you know the diameter of the Earth's orbit, you can calculate the distance to a nearby star by measuring its position at different times six months apart.

The farthest things

The most distant object ever seen is a quasar. Its light has taken about 12 billion years to reach us. The word "quasar" is short for "quasi-stellar object," meaning it looks like a star. But quasars are not stars, they are small, very energetic galaxies. A typical quasar emits about 10,000 times more light than our galaxy, but quasars are so far away that they appear as faint stars. Quasars are so hot that they emit X-rays and gamma rays as well as light.

▶ Even using very powerful telescopes, astronomers cannot make out much detail in an image of a quasar.

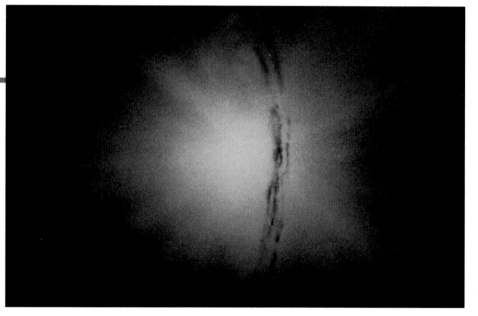

Globular clusters

Around the center of our galaxy, above and below the central bulge, are about 200 groups of stars, called globular clusters. These globular clusters are spherical, and the stars they contain are all the same age. They are as much as 300 light-years in diameter, and they are all orbiting around the center of the galaxy. The stars in globular clusters were born before the galaxy was properly formed, which means they are among the oldest stars known. The study of globular clusters is important to astronomy for many reasons. For example, knowing the age of the stars in globular clusters is important to scientists called cosmologists, who are trying to find out the age of our Universe. The age of stars in the globular clusters around our galaxy is about 15 billion years, which means that the Universe must be at least that old.

◀ A photograph of a typical globular cluster, taken through a powerful telescope, shows countless stars. There are more stars at the center of the cluster than at the edges.

STAR PROFILE

DEEP SPACE

If all stars gave out the same amount of light and were at the same distance from Earth, they would all look equally bright. But all stars are different, and some are much farther away than others.

The amount of light a star gives out every second is called its luminosity. A very hot star is more luminous than a cooler star of the same size. Just as heating a piece of metal makes it glow red-hot, then orange, then yellow, then white as its temperature increases, the temperature of a star can be worked out by its color. Really hot stars appear white or even bluish; cooler stars appear orange, yellow, or red. A star's size is important, too. If a large star and a small star are at the same temperature, the larger one will have a greater luminosity. The brightness of some stars varies for a number of reasons; some stars seem to switch on and off as they orbit each other in pairs.

Astronomers divide stars into different types. Most stars, including the Sun, are said to be in their main sequence —the middle of their lives. Stars at the end of their lives grow large, becoming red giants or red supergiants. Red giants eventually become small, hot stars—white dwarfs.

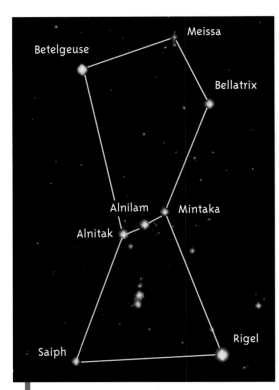

▲ Orion can be recognized in the night sky by a line of three bright stars—Orion's Belt.

Main sequence stars

The constellation Orion has several bright stars in their main sequence. Bellatrix and Rigel are large white-hot stars nearing the end of their main sequence, quickly burning themselves out. The stars of Orion's Belt—the three stars in a line—are all hot, white main sequence stars. The one at the right, called Mintaka, is much farther away than any of the other bright stars in Orion. Betelgeuse is a red supergiant star, past its main sequence, near the end of its life.

Charting the stars

To help sort out the different types of star, astronomers use the Hertzsprung-Russell diagram. The luminosity and temperature of a star decide its position on the chart. The hottest stars (blue or white) are to the left, while the coolest (orange or reddish) are to the right. Very luminous stars are at the top; the least luminous at the bottom. Large main sequence stars are hotter (to the left) and more luminous (farther up) than small ones (bottom right). So main sequence stars all lie on a diagonal line from top left to bottom right. Red giants are cool (far right), but their large size makes them very luminous (near the top). White dwarfs are hot (left of center) but their small size makes them less luminous (near the bottom).

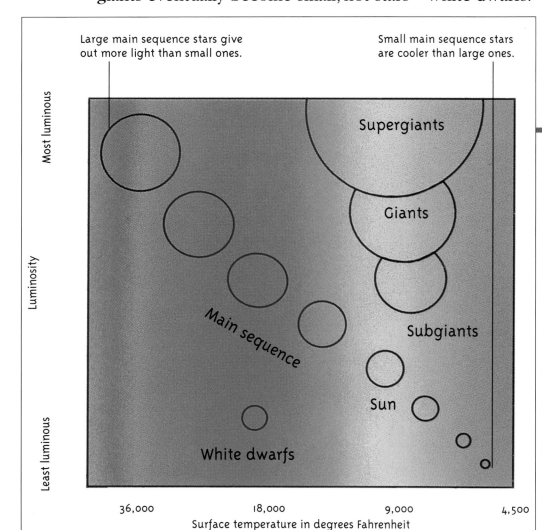

Large main sequence stars give out more light than small ones.

Small main sequence stars are cooler than large ones.

Supergiants

Giants

Main sequence

Subgiants

Sun

White dwarfs

| 36,000 | 18,000 | 9,000 | 4,500 |

Surface temperature in degrees Fahrenheit

Luminosity — Most luminous / Least luminous

◄ The Hertzsprung-Russell diagram. Our Sun is a yellowish main sequence star, near the middle of the diagonal line. It has an average luminosity.

Across the spectrum

The wires in an electric toaster glow red-hot—a phenomenon known as incandescence. If they were much hotter, they would also emit yellow light, and appear orange. Really hot objects emit light across the spectrum, from red to blue, appearing white. Stars produce light by incandescence, so astronomers can estimate a star's temperature by the color of its light. The temperature of an average yellow star like the Sun is about 11,000°F (6,000°C). The hottest stars have a surface temperature of about 54,000°F (30,000°C), and glow bluish-white.

Variable stars

Some stars become brighter or dimmer. Some of these "variable stars" are novas, which become brighter and stay that way. Most novas are exploding stars, at the end of their main sequence. Other variable stars become dimmer, then brighter again over a period of hours, days, or weeks. Rotating variables have some cooler regions on their surface, so they appear dimmer and brighter as they rotate. Another type of variable star is the eclipsing binary, which has a less luminous star orbiting it. When the second star passes in front of the first, we receive less light, so the star appears dimmer. Pulsating variables become brighter and dimmer because they are actually changing their size.

Double stars

To the naked eye, stars appear as single points of light, but through a telescope or binoculars, you can see that many of them are in fact two stars close together. These double, or binary, stars revolve around each other, held in their mutual (shared) orbit by the gravitational force between them. Mintaka, in Orion's Belt, is one example. Other double stars—called optical pairs—appear close together in the sky but are not in orbit around each other.

▲ A photograph of a typical double star, taken through a telescope

Star clusters

Stars are born in huge clouds of gas and dust called nebulas. Often, clusters of stars from the same nebula can be seen together. One of the best-known and most beautiful clusters is the Pleiades in the constellation Taurus. It is often called the Seven Sisters, because seven stars are visible to the naked eye. With a telescope, thousands more stars become visible.

▲ Betelgeuse, in Orion, is an example of a pulsating variable star, growing and shrinking every few years. It emits almost twice as much light when it is at its largest as when it is at its smallest.

◄ The Pleiades is a cluster of thousands of young stars, which illuminate the remains of the nebula in which they formed. Most nebulas give birth to hundreds or even thousands of stars.

49

THE BIRTH OF STARS

The space between the stars is not completely empty. It is filled with an extremely thin material called the interstellar medium. All stars—and the various planets, moons, asteroids, and comets that form around some of them—begin life as clumps of this material.

The interstellar medium consists almost entirely of the elements hydrogen and helium, but it is extremely thin—there is almost nothing there. In a liter of air on Earth there are more than 50 sextillion (a 5 with 22 zeroes) atoms or molecules. In a liter of interstellar medium there are only about 1,000 atoms. In some regions in space called molecular clouds, the concentration of atoms and molecules in the interstellar medium is much higher. There are thousands of these gigantic molecular clouds in our galaxy, each one made up of hydrogen molecules and helium atoms. Inside a molecular cloud, gravitational forces between the atoms and the molecules can pull the interstellar medium together, forming clumps that astronomers call protostars (forming stars). The material begins to heat up as gravity pulls the clump ever more tightly. Eventually, the center becomes so hot—several millions of degrees—that nuclear fusion begins to change the hydrogen into more helium, releasing enormous amounts of energy, and a star is born. Stars are being made like this all the time.

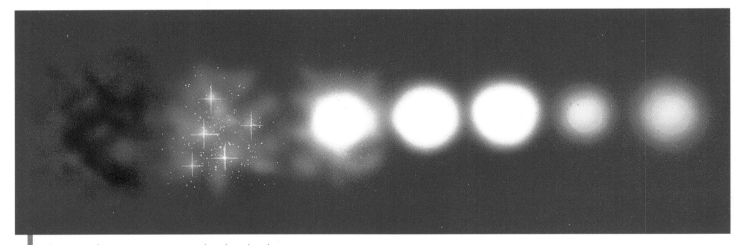

▲ Depending on its size, a molecular cloud may have enough material to make as few as ten or as many as several million stars.

Cloudy beginning

At first, a molecular cloud is dark. But as protostars begin to form inside it, the fusion reaction heats them from within, and they produce their own light, which illuminates the molecular cloud around them. The heat causes the pressure inside the protostar to increase, pushing out and balancing the force of gravity pulling in. Eventually, the star stops contracting, becoming stable and entering its main sequence. For a typical star, such as the Sun, the main sequence lasts about 10 billion years. In larger stars, the fusion reaction happens more quickly, and their main sequence is shorter. Really big stars shine for a only few hundred million years.

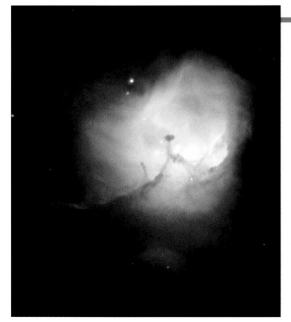

▲ New stars form inside a nebula. Radiation emitted by the young stars causes the nebula to glow.

Spinning stars

Star formation within a molecular cloud may be triggered by gas and dust from a nearby dying star. This disturbs the molecular cloud and sets it spinning, and as the protostars form, they too begin to spin. As the protostars shrink, they speed up—just as ice skaters spin faster by pulling their arms in toward their bodies. The shrinking protostar is often surrounded by a disk containing other clumps of the original molecular cloud, and these clumps may become planets orbiting the newborn star.

Pillars of creation

Space scientists have built up their knowledge of star formation by using their understanding of chemistry and physics, and by making clever observations of the light coming from or passing through molecular clouds. The Hubble Space Telescope has provided some amazing direct evidence to support the latest theories about star birth, including one of its most famously stunning photographs of space, taken in 1995. The photograph features a molecular cloud about 7,000 light-years away, in the Eagle Nebula in the constellation of Serpens (the Serpent). It shows the molecular cloud forming huge, dramatic pillar shapes as ultraviolet radiation coming from the new stars pushes it away. The largest pillar is about one light-year tall.

◀ One of the Hubble Space Telescope's most famous photographs shows the result of star birth in the Eagle Nebula.

Horsehead Nebula

One of the best-known views in space is the Horsehead Nebula, about 1,500 light-years away, in the constellation Orion. The shape that looks like a horse's head is a dark molecular cloud. The glorious red color behind it comes from hydrogen molecules in a nebula, which give out light as a result of radiation from a nearby star. The pale nebula below the red one reflects the light of a new star. The bright star on the left of the picture is the star at the left end of Orion's Belt.

▲ Many distant stars may have planets around them, like our Sun. Could any of them have life?

New planets

In 1995, astronomers found the first direct evidence of a planet around a star called 51 Pegasi, by measuring a "wobble" in the star's movement. The wobble was caused by the gravitational forces between the planet and the star. Since then, about 50 more planets have been discovered outside our own Solar System, using the same approach, and the Hubble Space Telescope has produced stunning photographs showing disks forming around protostars. Astronomers can even measure the mass of the planets—the heavier the planet, the greater the wobble.

▶ The Horsehead Nebula in the constellation Orion, with nearby stars, is a beautiful sight.

THE DEATH OF STARS

When a star comes to the end of its main sequence—when it can no longer convert hydrogen into helium at its core—it starts to cool down. What will happen next depends upon how big the star was in the first place.

The heat generated inside a main sequence star resists the crushing force of gravity. When the hydrogen runs out and nuclear fusion stops, gravity causes the star to shrink once more. Shrinking heats the star and starts up new nuclear reactions, making helium into elements such as oxygen and carbon. A typical star—like the Sun—will heat up and swell to become a red giant. Suddenly, it will throw off its outer layers, leaving a small, hot star—a white dwarf —that will fade away over millions of years. When a much bigger star runs out of hydrogen, it swells to become a supergiant. When a red supergiant stops producing energy, it ends its life in a huge explosion called a supernova, then settles to become a neutron star or a black hole.

▲ The red giant Sun, as seen from a hot, dry Earth, about 5 billion years from now

Future Sun

Our Sun is slowly becoming hotter. In about 3.5 billion years, it will be almost twice as bright as it is now. The water in Earth's oceans will evaporate, and Earth will be like Venus is today. In 5 billion years, the Sun will be a red giant about 200 times its current size, engulfing Mercury and Venus. Although the Sun's surface will be cooler, it will shine about 2,000 times more brightly. Finally, the Sun will swell and shrink several times before gradually shrinking and cooling to become a white dwarf star.

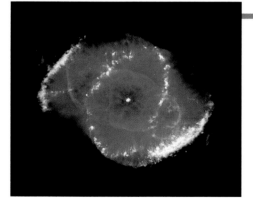

▲ The Cat's Eye Nebula, in Draco, is one of the most spectacular planetary nebulas.

The big push

Inside a dying star the size of the Sun, after the nuclear fusion has finished and the star has become a red giant, the core cools and shrinks to about the size of planet Earth. It leaves an enormous envelope of gases around it. The red giant pushes some of the envelope into space each time it swells and shrinks. The core is still hot enough to produce high-energy ultraviolet radiation, which slowly drives the envelope off into space. The envelope glows as ultraviolet radiation hits it. Astronomers call this a planetary nebula.

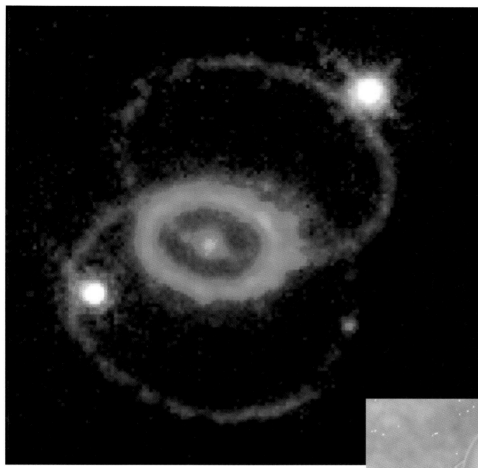

Out with a bang

From Earth, a supernova can be seen as a sudden dramatic brightening of a supergiant star. In 1987, astronomers had a rare opportunity to study a supernova as it was happening. The supernova, in the Large Magellanic Cloud—a small galaxy just outside our own Milky Way Galaxy—was the first to be witnessed since 1604. During a supernova, the supergiant's outer layers of gas are thrown far into space, leaving behind a tiny core. The matter of which the core is made becomes more and more crushed by gravity, until it is so dense that a cupful of it would have a mass of thousands of tons. At this stage, the core becomes a neutron star, just a few miles across.

◀ The remnants of a supernova 170,000 light-years away, photographed by the Hubble Space Telescope, show huge rings of material ejected into space.

◀ A massive star grows to become a supergiant, which finally explodes in a supernova and collapses to form a neutron star.

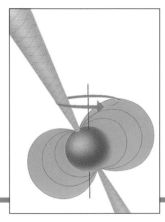

Spinning out

Most neutron stars spin, producing strong beams of radio waves. The beams shine out into space and can be detected by radio telescopes on Earth as rapid pulses. So spinning neutron stars are called pulsars. To date, more than 1,000 have been found.

◀ The magnetic field of a neutron star creates radio waves. The beams can be detected by radio telescopes.

▶ A molecular cloud contains elements from stars that have died, as well as hydrogen and helium created during the early Universe.

◀ Nothing can escape gravitational forces around a black hole, which actually "bend" the space around it.

Holes in space

Many massive stars will end life as a neutron star. But when a massive star's core shrinks to just a few miles in diameter, it becomes a black hole. The gravitational force surrounding a black hole is so strong that not even light can escape, so astronomers cannot see these strange objects directly. Instead, they see radiation coming from the space around the black hole, as matter from nearby stars is dragged into it.

Recycling in space

The material thrown into space during a supernova explosion is mostly hydrogen and helium, but contains other elements including carbon, oxygen, nitrogen, and iron. The explosion scatters these elements over a wide area, forming a thin veil of gas called a supernova remnant. This gas and dust adds to the interstellar medium in that part of space, and so can be absorbed into newly forming star systems. For example, the molecular cloud from which our Solar System formed contained material formed in a star that died long ago. Our planet—and even our bodies— are made from the material of dead stars.

GALAXIES

The Universe is enormous, and most of the galaxies that inhabit it are separated by unimaginable distances. Even the nearest galaxy to our own Milky Way Galaxy —the Andromeda Galaxy—is so far away that its light takes more than two million years to reach us. Through a small telescope, other galaxies look like fuzzy blobs. Until the 1920s, most astronomers believed that our own galaxy was the entire Universe, so they mistook the fuzzy blobs for nebulas inside the Milky Way.

In 1924, the American astronomer Edwin Hubble measured the distance to the Andromeda Galaxy, using the most powerful telescope available in the world at that time. His result provided conclusive proof that the nebula of Andromeda was actually a complete system of stars outside our own galaxy—and this came as a complete shock to many of the astronomers of the time.

Today, we can produce vivid images of these huge star systems, recognize the different types of galaxies, and learn about how they form and develop. And we can measure the distances to galaxies that are much farther than Edwin Hubble would have imagined. The study of other galaxies allows us to learn more about our own and to understand our place in space.

▲ The Hubble Deep Field View shows thousands of galaxies deep in space. Most of them are elliptical, but you can see other shapes, too.

Different shapes

There are billions of galaxies in the Universe. More than half of them are elliptical (egg-shaped). The farthest galaxies so far discovered are much farther away than the Andromeda Galaxy; their light has taken 12 billion years to reach us. In 1998, the Hubble Space Telescope took some amazing photographs of thousands of galaxies deep in space, by gazing in exactly the same direction for about 240 hours nonstop. For long periods of that time, the telescope's cameras collected light from a single tiny area of the sky, capturing some of the most distant galaxies ever seen.

▼ A spiral galaxy tilted toward us enables astronomers to work out its rotation and see detail in its disk.

Face-on or side-on

Spiral-shaped galaxies are of particular interest to astronomers. Side-on, a spiral galaxy is sausage-shaped with a bulge at the center. Astronomers can find how fast it rotates by measuring the speeds of stars on either side of the bulge—those on one side will be moving toward us, while those on the other will be moving away. When seen face-on, the areas of gas—in which new stars are being born—become visible. But elliptical galaxies look the same from any direction.

▲ Looking face-on at a spiral galaxy, we can see the wispy clouds of gas in which new stars are forming. The galaxy's bulge simply looks like a brighter patch at its center.

▲ Irregular galaxies have no particular shape. They have plenty of interstellar material (like spirals), but they have little or no rotation (like ellipticals). The type of galaxy shown here is called lenticular, which means "lens-shaped."

Types of galaxy

Hubble divided the galaxies he saw into three main types, according to their shapes: elliptical, spiral, and irregular. Elliptical galaxies, which are very common, contain mostly old stars of about the same age. Few new stars are born in elliptical galaxies, because they contain very few clumps of the interstellar medium from which new stars can form.

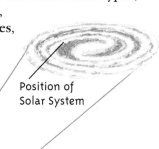

Position of Solar System

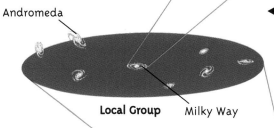

Andromeda

Local Group   Milky Way

◀ The Milky Way is near the center of the Local Group of galaxies, which is itself part of a much larger supercluster.

Position of Local Group in Local Supercluster

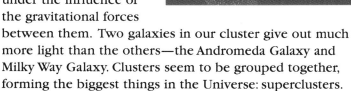

Clusters of galaxies

All the galaxies in the Universe are very far away, but about 30 are much closer than the rest. Together with our galaxy, they make up the Local Group—a cluster of galaxies all moving under the influence of the gravitational forces between them. Two galaxies in our cluster give out much more light than the others—the Andromeda Galaxy and Milky Way Galaxy. Clusters seem to be grouped together, forming the biggest things in the Universe: superclusters.

▲ Elliptical galaxies are egg-shaped or spherical. Although some of them have a slight rotation, they do not have arms or a central bulge like spiral galaxies. They contain only a little interstellar medium and consist mostly of old stars.

▲ Barred spirals are very similar to ordinary, disk-shaped spiral galaxies. They too rotate, and they too have stars of all ages. But their shape is slightly different—they have two huge straight "bars" extending out from the central bulge.

The Magellanic Clouds

The center of the Large Magellanic Cloud is 170,000 light-years away. The center of the Small Magellanic Cloud is 210,000 light-years away. Both are much closer than the Andromeda Galaxy—they give astronomers their best view of star birth and death in a galaxy outside our own. The two galaxies are in orbit around ours, just as the Moon is in orbit around Earth, and the Earth around the Sun. Both galaxies are easily visible to the naked eye in the southern hemisphere.

▲ Close-up of a globular cluster of stars in the Large Magellanic Cloud

Active galaxies

At the center of most galaxies lurks a massive black hole formed by the gravitational collapse of millions of stars. Black holes do not let light or other radiation escape. But when material falls into them, it heats up, producing radiation—some of which does escape. In some galaxies—active galaxies—a large amount of energy is released. Radio galaxies are active galaxies that look dim, but emit powerful beams of radio waves.

▲ About one in every 100 galaxies is an active galaxy.

◀ Radio galaxy (artist's impression)

THE BIG PICTURE

Cosmologists are scientists who ponder the really big questions in astronomy. To help them find answers, they use knowledge about the stars and galaxies gathered by astronomers (who observe things in space) and astrophysicists (who study the physical processes in stars and galaxies and in the space that separates them).

Astronomers have measured the sizes and distances of thousands of galaxies, and produced detailed three-dimensional charts showing how the galaxies are distributed in space. By measuring the speeds of thousands of galaxies, they have found out that nearly all galaxies are moving away from us, which suggests that space itself is expanding. Thanks to information like this, cosmologists have built up a clearer picture of the Universe. It seems that our Universe is very similar from wherever we look and in any direction we look. For example, there are no more galaxies in one direction than in another. There are still many great unsolved mysteries in cosmology. One is the missing mass problem: astronomers cannot detect as much matter as astrophysicists predict, based on current ideas about how the Universe works.

Moving away

In 1929, Edwin Hubble measured the distances to 29 other galaxies and the speeds at which they are moving through space. He was surprised to find that all the galaxies are moving away from us—suggesting that Earth is at the center of the Universe. But this is not necessarily so. Imagine yourself among a crowd of people. Now imagine that everyone starts to walk outward, making the crowd expand: everyone moves farther from everyone else. That is what is happening to the Universe: the space between the galaxies is expanding.

▲ As seen from Earth—or anywhere else in the Universe—all the galaxies are moving away from you as the space between them expands.

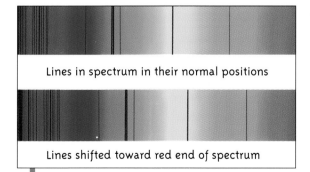

◀ The spectrum for a galaxy that is not moving away (top) and the red-shifted spectrum of a galaxy that is speeding away

Lines in spectrum in their normal positions

Lines shifted toward red end of spectrum

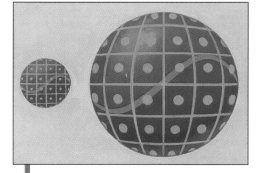

◀ It is useful to think of the Universe as a very slowly inflating balloon.

Red shift

Astronomers can measure the speed and direction of a galaxy by using something called red shift. If you produce a spectrum with light coming from a galaxy, you see dark lines across the colors. They correspond to particular chemical elements, which space scientists can recognize. When they look at the spectrum of a galaxy that is moving away from us, they see the lines are shifted along the spectrum toward the red end. The greater the red shift, the faster the galaxy is moving away.

Ballooning Universe

A rubber balloon has a closed surface—you could move your finger across it forever without coming to an edge. Astrophysicists believe that the Universe may be "closed" like this. Imagine that space is like a balloon being blown up. As it expands, markings on its surface move farther apart from each other. In the same way, the fact that galaxies are all receding is explained by the expansion of space between the galaxies.

Measuring distance

Edwin Hubble based his estimates of the distances to galaxies on observations of a particular type of star—a Cepheid variable. By charting its fluctuations (regular changes) in brightness, he could determine how luminous the star is (how much light it emits every second). Then, by comparing the star's luminosity to how bright it appears from Earth, he could figure out how far away it is. This method, developed by astronomer Henrietta Leavitt in 1912, is still used by astronomers to work out distances to galaxies today. Other methods include measuring the brightness of supernovas and the rotation speed of spiral galaxies.

◀ In 1994, the Hubble Space Telescope observed a Cepheid variable in this galaxy, called M101, which is 56 million light-years away.

Mapping the galaxies

In 2000, an international team of astronomers produced a map that looks like two slices of pizza. It shows where 100,000 galaxies are, out to a distance of 4 billion light-years, within the two slices of the sky. The map shows that galaxies are arranged in huge superclusters and that some superclusters are separated by empty spaces up to 200 million light-years wide. When the project is finished, it will provide astronomers with a way to measure the mass of the entire Universe.

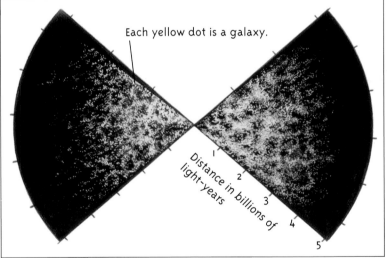

Each yellow dot is a galaxy.

Distance in billions of light-years

▲ Map of more than 100,000 galaxies, produced after two years of the 2dF Galaxy Redshift Survey, showing clusters and superclusters.

▲ The water tank at the Super-Kamiokande neutrino detector in Japan is about 130 feet (40 m) in diameter.

Missing mass

Current estimates for the total mass of objects in the Universe are much lower than cosmologists would predict. This is known as the missing mass problem. There are several theories to explain it. One idea is that much of the mass is carried by particles called neutrinos, which no telescope can pick up. A team of astronomers has found a way to catch neutrinos—in a huge tank of pure water surrounded by more than a thousand detectors.

Galactic distances and speeds

In 1929, Hubble found that the farther away a galaxy is, the faster it is moving away from us. Hubble discovered that dividing a galaxy's speed by its distance always gave approximately the same number, which cosmologists call the Hubble Constant.

Astronomers measure distances to galaxies in megaparsecs (Mpc). One Mpc is equal to 3.26 million light-years. The speed of a galaxy is measured in kilometers per second (km/s). Using these units, the Hubble Constant is about 80. Here are two examples:

● Galaxy NGC 55 is 2.3 Mpc away and is moving at 190 km/s. 190 divided by 2.3 gives 83.

● Galaxy NGC 4321 is 17.5 Mpc away and is moving at 1,400 km/s. 1,400 divided by 17.5 gives 80.

▶ All galaxies are speeding away from Earth.

THE BIG BANG

The ultimate quest for cosmologists is to find out how the Universe came to exist, how old it is, and what might happen to it far into the future. According to the most likely explanation for how the Universe began—the Big Bang Theory—all space, time, and matter were created when a tiny, incredibly energetic dot exploded about 15 billion years ago.

The Big Bang Theory was first put forward in 1931—two years after Edwin Hubble had discovered that the galaxies are all moving away. It was a Belgian priest called Georges Lemaître who first proposed the idea. He reasoned that if all the galaxies are moving away from each other, then at some time in the past they must all have been contained in a tiny space. In his mind, he wound back time and saw the galaxies collapsing together into a single point, which physicists call a singularity. Some of the energy in the singularity changed into matter, and space and time were born. The Universe expanded rapidly and then began to cool. After the heat from the Big Bang died down, helium and hydrogen nuclei—the central parts of helium and hydrogen atoms—began to form. Together with other particles, these went on to produce the first galaxies. The Big Bang would have produced an enormous amount of heat and radiation, and the Big Bang Theory predicts that astronomers should still be able to detect this as a faint radio signal.

The beginning of space and time

The singularity that exploded in the Big Bang had almost no size at all and yet contained all the energy in the Universe. All of a sudden, some of the energy changed into matter, and space expanded at an incredible rate. The newborn Universe grew to trillions of times its size in the tiniest fraction of a second and filled up with a superheated soup of subatomic particles (particles smaller than atoms). In minutes, protons and neutrons—particles found in the nuclei of atoms—had joined to form the first atomic nuclei.

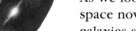

The Universe today

As we look out into space now, we see the galaxies still moving apart—the Universe is still expanding. We can also detect the echoes of the Big Bang in the radiation it created that is still traveling through space. New galaxies still continue to form, new stars are born, and old ones die. Our existence here on planet Earth is a tiny moment in the history of the Universe.

The first galaxies

About 300 million years after the Big Bang, the first galaxies began to form, in a network that stretches across unimaginably vast distances of space. The spaces between galaxies, where there is no matter at all, are called voids. The Universe continued expanding, and eventually stars began to shine.

Clumps of matter

Nuclei of the elements hydrogen and helium and a tiny amount of lithium, along with a dark matter that scientists do not yet understand, were created during the first three minutes of the Universe. Irregular distribution of this matter gradually caused it to clump together. From these clumps, galaxies eventually formed.

A cold end

In the far distant future, the Universe may continue to expand forever. The rate at which the Universe expands may slow down as gravitational force between all the galaxies pulls them back together. Depending on the total amount of matter in the Universe, the expansion may be too fast for gravity to stop it. The Universe may go on expanding forever.

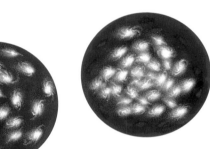

◀ Based on current estimates of the total mass of the Universe, the most likely future is that the galaxies will keep on moving apart, as space expands forever. If so, space will end up as a very cold, dark place.

The Big Crunch

The Universe could end as it began. Cosmologists call this idea the Big Crunch. In this scenario, there is enough matter in the Universe for gravity to slow its expansion and to start the galaxies moving toward each other. Eventually, all the matter would collapse into a singularity, and the entire Universe and all its history would be lost.

▼ Arno Penzias and Robert Wilson standing in front of the radio antenna that first detected the cosmic background radiation

Cosmic background radiation

The Big Bang Theory was controversial throughout the 1940s and 1950s, but began to gain more support in the 1960s. In America in 1965, two physicists—Arno Penzias and Robert Wilson—picked up a faint radio signal coming from space. The radio waves seemed to come from every direction. After ruling out any other option, Penzias and Wilson realized that the radio waves were the echoes of the intense radiation produced by the Big Bang. This cosmic background radiation is convincing evidence in favor of the Big Bang Theory, fitting its predictions very well.

Ripples in spacetime

The radiation that Penzias and Wilson detected with their large ground-based radio antenna seemed exactly the same in every part of the sky. But for galaxies to form, there had to have been tiny irregularities in the radiation produced after the Big Bang. So, in 1989, NASA launched COBE—the Cosmic Background Explorer. The spacecraft orbited Earth, pointing its sensitive instruments in every part of the sky. The COBE spacecraft produced detailed maps that showed variations in the cosmic background radiation, in exact agreement with the Big Bang Theory.

North celestial hemisphere   South celestial hemisphere

-100 μK   +100 μK

◀ COBE sky maps of the north and south celestial hemispheres, which reflect variations in temperature in the early Universe. The variations are minute and are measured in micro-Kelvins (μK).

SPACE EXPLORATION

If you tried to travel into space in a jet plane, you would not get very far. Jet engines need to take in air to supply oxygen to burn their fuel, and there is no air in space. The altitude record for a jet plane is about 12 miles (20 km), and space begins at an altitude of about 60 miles (100 km). A rocket engine carries its own supply of oxygen, so that it can burn fuel even in space.

Some rockets actually carry liquid oxygen, together with liquid fuel, normally hydrogen. Solid-fuel rockets use fuel that is made of pellets, which contain a combustible chemical (one that burns well) mixed with a chemical compound, called an oxidizer, that contains oxygen. As well as being able to burn fuel where there is no air, rockets that carry spacecraft into space must be very powerful. To reach low Earth orbit, a rocket must travel at about 5 miles per second (8 km/s); to escape from Earth's gravity, its speed must be more than 7 miles per second (11 km/s). Any less than this, and the rocket will be pulled back down to Earth again. Rockets burn fuels rapidly in their engines, producing hot gases that escape at high speed through a nozzle at the bottom. The downward motion of the exhaust gases exerts a force upward on the rocket, in the same way as air escaping from a balloon makes it fly quickly in the opposite direction. Rockets do not travel straight up into space—they shoot into orbit around the Earth. Many spacecraft remain in orbit, kept there by gravity, in the same way as the Moon orbits Earth. Other spacecraft use booster engines to move to a new orbit or—if they are bound for the Moon or the planets—far out into space. Despite their success, rocket engines have disadvantages. They are very heavy and very expensive, and they quickly run out of fuel. New ways of getting into space may overcome these disadvantages.

Traveling in stages

Most rockets are designed in sections, called stages, each one with its own engines. The first stage rocket is the biggest, because it has to lift the weight of the entire rocket and its fuel off the ground. Once the rocket is several miles in the air, the fuel of the first stage is used up, and the smaller, second stage takes over to take the rest of the rocket out of the atmosphere. Most rockets have a third stage or even a fourth that positions the spacecraft into its orbit.

First stage

Second stage

Third stage

Payload

▲ Each part of a staged rocket is smaller than the previous one, because it has less work to do—there is less weight to carry, and the spacecraft is already traveling at speed. The final stage carries the payload—a satellite or a crewed module—into orbit.

Rocket man

One of the pioneers of rocket design was German engineer Werner von Braun. During World War II, he headed a top secret group making missiles for the German Army. His brainchild was the V-2, first launched in 1942. After the war, the Americans and Russians captured a large number of V-2s and used them as the basis of their rocket development programs. Von Braun became an American citizen and was chief designer to several American rockets, including the Saturn V, which first launched people on their way to the Moon.

◀ Werner von Braun (1912-1977)

Soviet rocket

Proton rockets were introduced in 1965 and quickly became the standard launch vehicles for the Soviet space effort. They can be used in a three- or four-stage configuration, depending on the weight of payload and the orbit required. The rocket is very powerful, with six large booster rockets attached to the side of the first stage. Protons are still used for national, international, and commercial launches. They ferry heavy parts up to the International Space Station, as well as launching communications satellites.

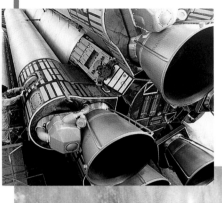

◀ The huge boosters on the Soviet Proton rocket help to make it a popular choice for several different types of space mission.

▼ The International Space Station in orbit around Earth

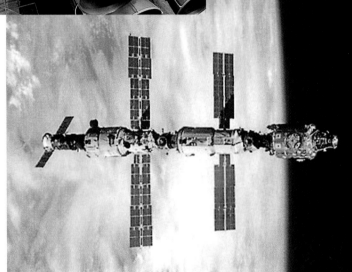

▶ Launch of an Ariane 5 rocket from Kourou, French Guiana

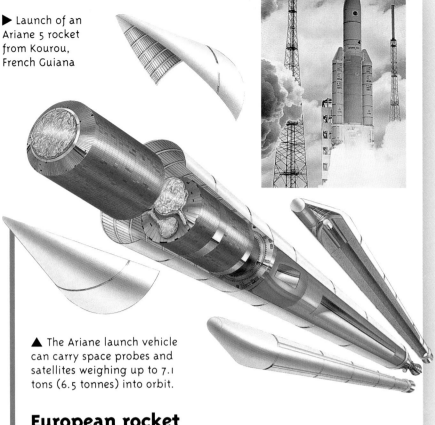

▲ The Ariane launch vehicle can carry space probes and satellites weighing up to 7.1 tons (6.5 tonnes) into orbit.

European rocket

In the early days of spaceflight, the United States and the Soviet Union competed in a "space race." Their governments spent vast sums of money trying to be the first into space. But several other countries now have space agencies, and in 1980, the first commercial space organization was formed. This company—Arianespace—launches up to half of all the satellites sent into orbit each year, most carried aboard the Ariane rocket. Arianespace launches its rockets from a site in Kourou, French Guiana, in South America.

Rocket launches

Most launch sites for rockets are near to Earth's equator. This is because the spin of the planet there gives extra push to the rocket as it propels itself into space. After a long countdown, during which engineers carry out many tests, the rocket blasts off, lifting slowly at first. Burning about a ton of fuel every second for the first few minutes after launch, the rocket accelerates to a speed of about 4 miles (7 km) per second after just four minutes. After about nine minutes, it achieves its first Earth orbit and can then be propelled to a different orbit or out into space.

▶ Rockets, such as this Delta II, are very heavy. Even though their engines are very powerful, they move slowly at first.

New rockets

The greater the mass of exhaust gas thrown out every second by a rocket engine, and the faster it is pushed out, the greater the thrust. So a rocket that expels gases at much higher speed can achieve the same thrust using much less fuel. This is the idea behind the ion drive, a rocket engine being tested by NASA. Electricity generated by solar panels creates ions—electrically charged atoms—and then expels them at nearly the speed of light.

▼ NASA's Deep Space 1 uses an ion drive rocket engine.

Off the rails

In the future, small spacecraft could be launched from Earth orbit—or from the ground—using electricity and magnetism rather than chemical fuels. A railgun is a long metal tube that uses electromagnetic forces to propel objects to extremely high speeds. Railguns that were permanently in orbit around the Earth could provide the thrust to propel very small, cheap space probes to the planets.

▲ Small probes could be launched by railgun.

PEOPLE ON THE MOON

SPACE EXPLORATION

The Moon is a glorious sight in our sky, but can you imagine what the Earth must look like from the Moon? Twelve people have actually stood on the Moon's surface and gazed back at Earth. They were all American astronauts.

The first person to make it into space was a Soviet astronaut, Yuri Gagarin. In April 1961, he orbited the Earth for nearly two hours before returning safely to Earth. The Soviet Union had moved ahead in the space race—a huge embarrassment for the American space program. Just six weeks later, the U.S. President John F. Kennedy announced that the United States intended to land a person on the Moon by the end of the 1960s. As a result, the American space agency, NASA, set up the *Apollo* program, and in July 1969, an *Apollo* spacecraft landed on the Moon's surface. Astronaut Neil Armstrong became the first person ever to set foot there. His famous words, "This is one small step for man, one giant leap for mankind," were supposed to begin with, "This is one small step for a man." Landing people on the Moon certainly was a remarkable achievement, but whether or not it was a giant leap for humankind remains an unanswered question; no one has been back there since 1972. The astronauts who ventured onto the surface took stunning photographs, collected samples of rock and regolith (lunar soil), carried out hundreds of experiments, and were treated to the unforgettable sight of their beautiful blue-and-white home planet rising and setting in the lunar sky.

▶ The *Apollo* spacecraft that left Earth was much heavier than the one that parachuted back (the Command Module).

▲ Three possible approaches to the *Apollo* mission

Making it possible

Apollo missions involved leaving a spacecraft in orbit around the Moon while a lighter craft visited the surface (3). NASA considered two other approaches, with the whole spacecraft landing on the Moon. This involved carrying much more fuel from Earth. No rocket would be powerful enough to do this alone (1), and sending a second rocket with the extra fuel (2) would have been impractical and expensive.

The Lunar Module

The main bulk of the *Apollo* spacecraft—the Command and Service Modules—remained in lunar orbit, while a smaller craft —called the Lunar Module—landed on the Moon's surface. The Lunar Module was designed to reduce the need for fuel to a minimum. The lower half of the Lunar Module (the Descent Stage) was only needed to ensure a soft landing on the Moon's surface. So, to reduce the amount of fuel needed, only the small part at the top (the Ascent Stage) lifted off the Moon again, to meet with the Command and Service Modules.

◀ The *Apollo* Lunar Module had an Ascent Stage and a Descent Stage.

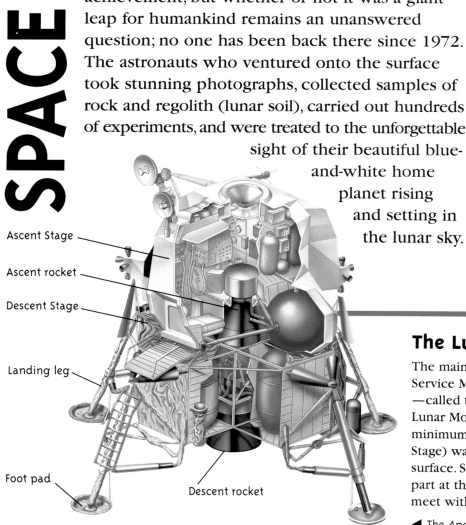

Ascent Stage

Ascent rocket

Descent Stage

Landing leg

Foot pad

Descent rocket

There and back

The total mass of the *Apollo* spacecraft at launch, including the huge Saturn V rocket, was about 3,200 tons (2,910 tonnes). The only part that made it back to Earth eight days later was the Command Module.

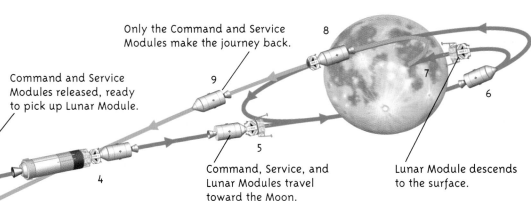

Command and Service Modules released, ready to pick up Lunar Module.

Only the Command and Service Modules make the journey back.

Third stage of Saturn V rocket pushes the modules on their way to the Moon.

Command, Service, and Lunar Modules travel toward the Moon.

Lunar Module descends to the surface.

2 3 4 5 6 7 8 9 10

On the approach to Earth, the Command Module separated from the Service Module.

Moon missions

The biggest achievement of the *Apollo* program took place in 1969, when Neil Armstrong first stepped out onto the Moon's surface from the *Apollo 11* Lunar Module. But there were other important missions, too. *Apollo 8*, for example, was the first crewed mission to reach the Moon, in 1968. During *Apollo 15*, *16*, and *17*, astronauts drove a specially designed car called the Lunar Rover, making it easier to travel greater distances across the surface.

The *Apollo* missions

	Landed	Crew members	Time out of Module	Distance covered	Mass of sample
11	July 20, 1969	Armstrong, Aldrin, Collins	2 hrs 32 min	820 ft	48 lbs
12	Nov 19, 1969	Conrad, Bean, Gordon	7 hrs 45 min	4,430 ft	76 lbs
13	(No landing)	Lovell, Swigert, Haise	-	-	-
14	Feb 5, 1971	Shepard, Mitchell, Roosa	9 hrs 23 min	11,320 ft	95 lbs
15	July 30, 1971	Scott, Irwin, Worden	19 hrs 8 min	17 miles	169 lbs
16	Apr 21, 1972	Young, Duke, Mattingly	20 hrs 14 min	17 miles	209 lbs
17	Dec 11, 1972	Cernan, Schmitt, Evans	22 hrs 4 min	22 miles	244 lbs

▲ View through Lunar Module window

◄ An offshoot of the *Apollo* program, called *Apollo* orbiting observatory

▲ Buzz Aldrin and the American flag on the Moon during *Apollo 11*

Some Moon facts from *Apollo*

- The youngest surface rocks were formed 3.2 billion years ago— so there has been no general volcanic activity since that time.
- The Moon's crust is less dense than the Earth's—so the two bodies have a different composition.
- Early in its history the Moon was covered with hot lava tens of miles deep, evidently caused by the energy from impacts.
- Only a small core about 900 miles (1,500 km) in diameter is molten (liquid). Earth has a much larger liquid core.

Apollo 13

On April 11, 1970, the third mission bound for the lunar surface set off across the 240,000-mile (375,000-km) gap between the Earth and the Moon. Two days into the mission, *Apollo 13* hit trouble—an electrical short circuit caused a series of problems, including an explosion in one of the oxygen tanks and loss of most electrical power. Three astronauts, in a tiny metal container far away from home, abandoned their mission, continued around the Moon, and managed to return safely to Earth.

◄ The *Apollo 13* story was made into a film of the same name, starring Tom Hanks as Commander James Lovell.

REUSABLE SPACECRAFT

During the launch of a spacecraft, large parts of the rocket fall off and are lost in space. Sending rockets into space would be much cheaper if spacecraft could be used again. A reusable spacecraft would need to stay in one piece from launch until landing, with only a refueling between missions.

There is already a spacecraft that has some reusable parts, the Space Shuttle. The part of the spacecraft that carries the crew and the cargo is called the orbiter. After each mission, it returns to Earth and can be used again. The first Space Shuttle was launched in 1981, and 20 years later just five orbiter vehicles had notched up 100 launches. Two separate solid fuel rocket engines, which help to accelerate the orbiter upward, fall back to Earth during the launch to be recovered and reused, but a large external tank is lost during each launch.

The next generation of space launchers will be Single Stage to Orbit rockets—completely reusable. NASA is developing one, called VentureStar, which will be the successor to the Space Shuttle. Even private companies are becoming involved in the quest for cheaper space travel. The X-prize is a competition that offers a huge financial reward to the designers of a rocket system that is able to make space accessible to more people, perhaps opening up the way to space tourism.

The orbiter separates from its fuel tank once it has reached its orbit.

Back to Earth

After up to 17 days in orbit, the Space Shuttle orbiter is positioned for reentry into Earth's atmosphere—with its engines facing forward. The spacecraft hits the atmosphere at high speed, generating tremendous amounts of heat as it rubs against the air. The nose and the bottom surface of the orbiter are covered with heat-resistant tiles that can withstand temperatures of 2,700°F (1,500°C). After its reentry, the orbiter glides to Earth and lands on an airfield like an airplane.

▼ The Shuttle orbiter is followed by a chase plane as it glides back to Earth.

Boosters jettisoned

Space Shuttle

On the launch pad, the Space Shuttle orbiter sits vertically, attached to its fuel tank and solid fuel boosters. After the launch, at an altitude of 28 miles (45 km), the fuel in the boosters is all used up. They are released from the orbiter and drop into the sea. A recovery team collects them so that they can be used again. Once the orbiter reaches its orbit, the fuel tank is no longer needed. It falls back toward Earth and burns up as it passes through the upper atmosphere.

Lift-off from launch pad

▶ On the launch pad, the Space Shuttle stands as tall as a seven-story building.

▲ The orbiter—the part of the spacecraft that carries the crew—is slowed down by parachutes on landing.

In orbit, the Space Shuttle orbiter travels at speeds of up to 17,500 miles per hour (28,000 km/h) and at an altitude between 115 and 620 miles (185–1,000 km). The view is spectacular.

The Space Shuttle at work

The Space Shuttle's payloads—carried inside the huge payload bay—include commercial and military satellites, space probes, and parts for the International Space Station. Most are deployed (released) by a long robotic arm controlled by the crew. In 1990, the orbiter *Discovery* carried the Hubble Space Telescope into space and released it in this way. Since then, several Space Shuttle crews have returned to the space telescope to carry out servicing and repairs. Most Space Shuttle missions also carry several scientific experiments that are carried out in orbit.

Space Shuttle facts

- Orbiter: length 122 feet (37.2 m), wingspan 78 ft (23.8 m), diameter 15 feet (4.5 m), mass 109 tons.
- Solid fuel boosters: length 126 feet (38.5 m), mass when empty 95 tons, mass of solid fuel 550 tons.
- Liquid fuel tank: length 154 feet (46.9 m), mass when empty 33 tons, mass of liquid fuel 795 tons.
- Total mass of Space Shuttle on launch pad: 1,590 tons.
- Orbiters and their first flights: *Enterprise* (test vehicle only), *Columbia* (1981), *Challenger* (1983), *Discovery* (1984), *Atlantis* (1985), *Endeavor* (1992).

▲ The orbiter's main engines ▲ On the launch pad

Disaster!

Only one Space Shuttle has failed, but the moment of failure was a tragic one that shocked the whole world. It happened in January 1986, on the ninth mission of the orbiter named *Challenger*. Burning gas escaped out of a seal on one of the solid rocket boosters and broke the huge liquid fuel tank, releasing liquid hydrogen. Just 73 seconds after launch and in front of millions watching on television, the liquid hydrogen blew up in a huge explosion, killing all seven astronauts aboard and destroying the satellite the orbiter was carrying.

▲ The *Challenger* Space Shuttle disaster shocked the world.

▲ Artist's impression of VentureStar

The next step

VentureStar will be the first fully reusable spacecraft. Unlike Space Shuttles, it does not need a huge external fuel tank or separate booster rockets, so everything that goes up will come down again. Its shape, called a "lifting body," will enable it to glide back to Earth even though it has no wings. It will not carry crew or passengers, but it should dramatically reduce the cost of putting a commercial or military payload into space. The X-33 is a half-size test model of VentureStar, which is due for launch in 2003.

The X-prize

The $10-million prize money offered by the X-prize Foundation will be given to the first team that flies its spacecraft to an altitude of 60 miles (100 km) twice in 14 days. Each design must be able to carry three adults into space and back. The entries range from space planes like the Shuttle orbiter to more conventional rockets.

▲ One of the X-prize entries, the XVan2001, will use jet engines for the ascent, switching to rockets in space.

65

WORKING IN SPACE

SPACE EXPLORATION

More than 400 people have been into space so far. The earliest human space flights achieved important goals of exploration, such as landing people on the Moon. These missions paved the way for people to work in space. But what kind of work do astronauts carry out?

Space Shuttle missions often launch or repair commercial satellites. The astronauts aboard a Space Shuttle orbiter have to be able to deploy satellites using the remote manipulator, the orbiter's huge robotic arm. The Hubble Space Telescope was deployed in this way and has been repaired or serviced several times during Space Shuttle missions. During servicing missions, astronauts had to go outside the orbiter and float free in space to work on the telescope. The time spent outside a spacecraft is called extravehicular activity (EVA), or a space walk. During a space walk, a space suit protects the astronaut against impact from flying pieces of dust or fragments of other spacecraft, and from harmful radiation from the Sun. It must also supply the astronaut pressurized oxygen and keep him or her at the right temperature.

As well as deploying and servicing satellites, astronauts often have to carry out scientific experiments, many of which take advantage of the conditions in orbit. Many of the experiments involve microgravity, the fact that everything in space—including the astronauts themselves— behaves as if it is weightless.

▶ Ed White making the first space walk by an American, in June 1965.

▼ Like all early spacewalkers, White was tethered to his spacecraft.

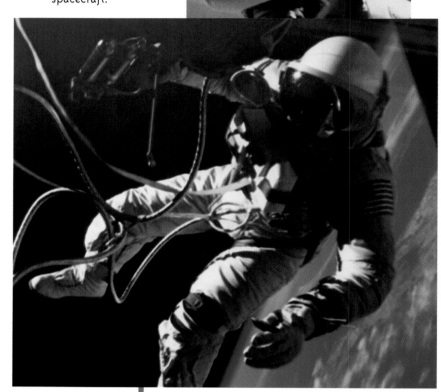

Floating free

The first person to make a space walk was Soviet astronaut Alexei Leonov, who went outside his *Voshkod 2* spacecraft for more than 10 minutes in March 1965. He was tethered (attached) to his spacecraft by tubes that supplied him with oxygen and prevented him from floating away. Today's spacewalkers float free, with their own oxygen supply and a jet pack to move around. Space suits for EVA around the International Space Station can be used up to 25 times before being refurbished.

Dangerous activity

The first person in space was Soviet astronaut Yuri Gagarin. His orbit of Earth in 1961, in the spacecraft *Vostok 1*, nearly ended in disaster. During reentry, wires holding the two parts of the craft together failed to let go, and the craft began to spin wildly out of control. After ten agonizing minutes, the wires vaporized (became gas) in the intense heat of reentry, releasing Gagarin in his metal sphere, from which he made a planned parachute jump back to the ground.

◀ Yuri Gagarin, courageous space explorer

Some space records

- First astronaut: Yuri Gagarin (USSR), April 12, 1961.
- First woman astronaut: Valentina Tereshkova (USSR), June 16, 1963.
- Fastest astronauts: the *Apollo 10* crew (Cernan, Stafford, and Young) reached a speed of 7 miles/sec (11.1 km/s) during reentry on May 26, 1969.
- Farthest distance from Earth: the *Apollo 13* crew (Lovell, Swigert, and Haise) reached a distance of 249,204 miles (401,056 km) on April 14, 1970.
- Longest time in space: Valeri Polyakov (USSR) spent 438 days in *Mir*, starting on January 10, 1994.

◀ Valentina Tereshkova, the first woman in space, is pictured on a Czechoslovakian stamp.

▶ EVA astronauts have to carry all the tools they need with them and are in constant radio contact with their ground control.

◀ Experiment to find out how seeds grow in microgravity

▶ If astronauts can grow plants in microgravity, they can grow their own food.

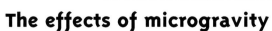

The effects of microgravity

In 1983, a European laboratory called *Spacelab* was carried into orbit by the Space Shuttle. *Spacelab* was launched several times until its final mission in 1997. Astronauts used it for hundreds of scientific experiments, many on the effects of microgravity. One involved watching how flames develop without gravity—work that is important in designing rocket engines. The effects of microgravity on humans have been studied in great detail, as have its effects on the development of seeds and animals' eggs.

Catching satellites

The Space Shuttle missions are so regular that space walks have become routine. Space Shuttle astronauts are trained to carry out space walks in large water tanks like deep swimming pools. The Space Shuttle orbiter can maneuver itself into the same orbit as any satellite to an altitude of 600 miles (1,000 km) and change its speed to make a soft docking. Astronauts can then go out to the satellite and make repairs. Outside the orbiter, astronauts wear an extravehicular mobility unit (EMU).

▼ Astronaut with EMU servicing the Hubble Space Telescope

They paid with their lives. . .

- January 27, 1967: three *Apollo* astronauts (Chaffee, Grissom, and White) died when a fire broke out in a Command Module they were testing on the ground. They could not open the escape hatch.
- April 23, 1967: the USSR astronaut Alexei Komarov died when the parachute of his *Soyuz 1* craft failed to open. This disaster led to the cancellation of the Soviet lunar-orbit program.
- January 28, 1986: a crew of seven died when the *Challenger* Shuttle exploded soon after takeoff. The design flaw that caused the crash took two years to fix.

▲ Disaster struck Space Shuttle *Challenger* in 1986.

LIVING IN SPACE

Space is a harsh environment. If human beings stepped out of a spacecraft unprotected, all the air would rush out of their lungs in a split second, and they would die almost instantly. Harmful radiation from the Sun is always present, and there is nothing there to eat or drink. How do space flight engineers keep astronauts alive in these conditions?

During their time in space, astronauts are protected against the Sun's radiation by a metal shell called a capsule. Inside this cramped, isolated capsule, life-support systems must provide oxygen for the astronauts to breathe in, filter out the carbon dioxide they breathe out, and maintain a comfortable temperature. The capsule must also provide them with light and electrical power, food and drink, somewhere to sleep, and a toilet.

Perhaps the most obvious difference between life in space and life on Earth is the feeling of weightlessness. But it is not true that there is no gravity in orbit. In fact, without gravity, there would be no orbit: the spacecraft and its astronauts would fly off into space. The reason astronauts feel weightless is that they and their spacecraft are in orbit together. During long space missions, weightlessness can cause bones to weaken. There is no way that people can go for long walks or run around in a space capsule, so it is important for astronauts to take regular exercise.

▲ Weightlessness can be fun.

What is weightlessness?

If you were standing in an elevator at the top of a tall building and the cable snapped, you and the elevator car would fall together. You would feel weightless as you lost contact with the floor. Astronauts are trained for weightlessness in just this way. They ride in airplanes that climb to a high altitude, then dive in free fall. While the plane is diving, astronauts learn what it will feel like to be in space. Weightlessness means that there is no up or down, so anything that is not secured can float about the cabin.

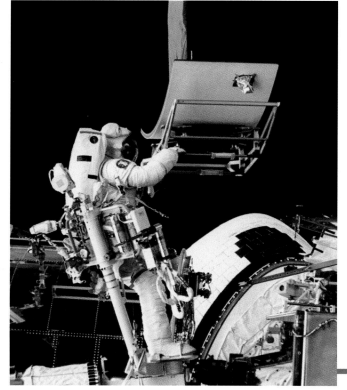

◀ Space Shuttle astronauts breathe pure oxygen when performing any extravehicular activity.

Breathing in space

We breathe because our bodies need a constant supply of oxygen. On Earth, oxygen makes up nearly one-quarter of the atmosphere. Early space capsules were filled with pure oxygen at a lower pressure than on Earth, but after a raging fire destroyed the first *Apollo* mission on the launch pad, killing all its crew, this practice was stopped. Modern capsules are filled with "synthetic air," an artificial mixture of gases similar to the atmosphere. Astronauts still breathe pure oxygen inside space suits during space walks.

Space clothes

Shuttle crews have three sets of clothes:

- A special suit for ascent and descent. This includes a parachute and emergency equipment to support them for up to 24 hours in a life raft.
- For everyday wear—comfortable, flame-retardant clothes with plenty of closable pockets.
- A space suit, which they use for extravehicular activity. There is one design of suit for both men and women. Modern suits are in two pieces that snap together at the waist, sealing in pressurized oxygen. The upper half is of fiberglass and contains the oxygen supply.

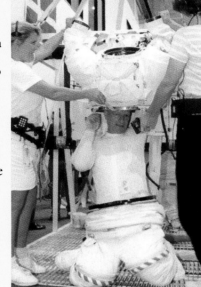

▶ Space Shuttle astronaut being helped on with his space suit during pre-flight training

Space hygiene

Using the toilet in space is a very awkward business. The toilet itself has a suction effect that draws in human waste, preventing it from floating around in the capsule. The solid waste is dried and stored, then returned to Earth for disposal, while urine is stored and occasionally released out into space with other waste water. The waste water is propelled downward, so that it can become part of the atmosphere. No spacecraft has ever carried a washing machine—dirty clothes are put into bags and returned to Earth.

▲ Inside the Space Shuttle's toilet cubicle. The astronaut grasps one of the handholds—just beyond him, you can see the toilet seat.

▲ All the food aboard space missions is brought from Earth, so weight is crucial.

Eating and drinking

The food eaten by astronauts in early space missions was far from appetizing. Most of it was either in powder or paste form or was stored as bite-sized cubes. Today's astronauts have a much better menu, though much of their food is still powdered and has to be rehydrated (have water added) in the spacecraft. Some crewed missions make their own water (H_2O) for this by combining hydrogen (H) and oxygen (O) in fuel cells that also produce electrical power. Crumbs are not welcome in a spacecraft, because they float around in the capsule.

Keeping healthy

Weightlessness has been found to have many effects on the human body. All astronauts have to be fit, but a long stay in space can be a challenge even for them.

- The heart and other muscles get out of condition, because they do not have enough to do.
- "Motion sickness," partly due to the way the blood circulates through the body, is a common problem.
- Human bones naturally lose and gain calcium, but in space they lose more than they gain.

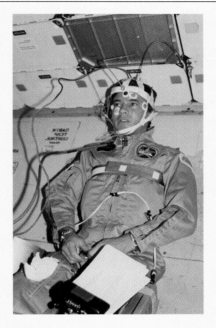

▶ An astronaut in space measures his heart and breathing rate, brain activity, and blood pressure.

Full life support

The ultimate in space suits is the manned maneuvering unit (MMU), which is like a personal spacecraft. It has toilet facilities in the form of a strong diaper, life-support systems—oxygen supply and temperature stabilization— and its own radio and video camera for communications. And, just like a spacecraft, it is able to propel itself around. The astronaut controls his or her position and speed using nozzles that release jets of nitrogen gas. There are 24 different nozzles at different angles, giving the astronaut good control over the speed and direction of travel.

▲ A well-equipped astronaut with an MMU, in orbit about 200 miles (300 km) above Earth's surface, traveling at a speed of about 6 miles per second (10 km/s).

69

SATELLITES AT WORK

SPACE EXPLORATION

Any object in orbit around another object is a satellite. Until the dawn of the space age, Earth had only one satellite, the Moon. The space age began with the launch of the first artificial satellite, *Sputnik 1*, on October 4, 1957. Since then, Earth has gained thousands of artificial satellites.

Artificial satellites communicate with radio antennas on Earth by sending and receiving radio signals. Some relay telephone calls or television pictures; others send views of cloud cover to help weather forecasters. Some are scientific satellites that help astronomers study space from above our atmosphere or help Earth scientists study Earth from space. Navigation satellites such as those in the Global Positioning System (GPS) help us work out our position on Earth with great accuracy.

All satellites are launched into space by rockets, then made to travel at carefully calculated speeds and in precise directions so that they achieve the right orbit for their job. Every satellite has a way of remaining stable and some way of changing its direction and speed if necessary. Not all artificial satellites are useful. Space is becoming crowded— with rocket engines discarded after launch, small parts of spacecraft that have fallen off, and satellites that have come to the end of their lives.

Communications satellites

When you watch a television program broadcast from another country, the signals have probably been bounced off a satellite in space. Communications satellites relay thousands of TV channels and handle millions of telephone conversations every day. Most communications satellites are directly above the equator in geostationary orbit. This orbit takes exactly one day to complete, the same amount of time Earth takes to rotate once, so a satellite in geostationary orbit is always above the same point on Earth's surface. This makes it easy for people on the ground to tune into its signals.

What's inside a satellite?
- The bus: a rigid framework that holds everything together during launch and in space.
- An electrical power supply: this usually uses energy from solar panels to recharge storage batteries.
- A computer to keep the systems operating.
- A radio transmitter and receiver for communication with ground control.
- An ACS (Attitude Control System) to stop the satellite from tumbling out of control.
- If it is a communications satellite it will contain transponders, which amplify the signals received from the ground before transmitting them back to Earth again.

Antenna — Solar panel

◀ A typical satellite

◀ Weather satellite image of cloud cover over North America, superimposed on a map

Weather satellites

Modern weather forecasting depends on the pictures and other information collected by weather satellites. Television cameras attached to a weather satellite beam down images that may appear directly on the Internet. The images also enable meteorologists (weather scientists) to track hurricanes, so that people in danger can be warned. Most weather satellites are in polar orbits, close enough to the Earth to produce detailed pictures. They pass over the North and South Poles, which play important roles in the weather.

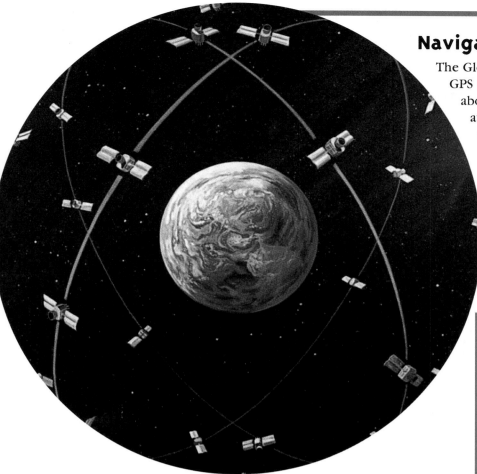

Navigation satellites

The Global Positioning System (GPS) allows people with GPS receivers to learn where on Earth they are—within about 100 yards. The receiver picks up signals from at least three of 24 GPS satellites which orbit at an altitude of about 6,800 miles (11,000 km). By measuring tiny differences in the time the signals arrive, a microchip in the receiver can calculate its position almost exactly. Some cars are outfitted with GPS receivers and can plot a driver's location on a detailed street map.

◄ The satellites of the Global Positioning System circle the Earth at 6,800 miles (11,000 km).

▼ Map showing the amount of space junk around Earth. Each dot is a piece of debris bigger than a tennis ball.

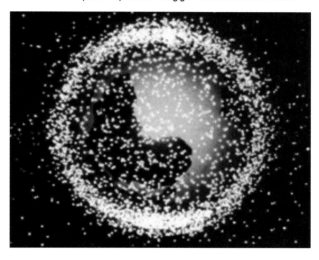

Remote sensing satellites

Earth scientists study a wide range of features of our planet, such as rock formations, the growth of deserts, and the changing course of rivers. Some study pollution from industrial areas running into the sea. Some are looking for patterns in land use—they need to know how much of a particular country is countryside, or how much is urban (cities), for example. Remote sensing satellites can help enormously with all these tasks, and can also help to produce accurate maps of anywhere on Earth.

◄ Satellite image of New York, taken by the Landsat 5 satellite

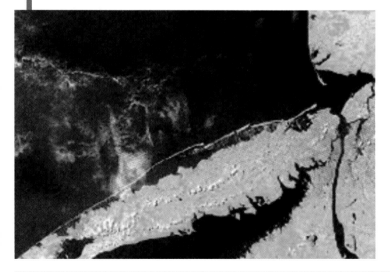

Space junk

In addition to the 5,000 or so satellites, there are tens of thousands of pieces of debris bigger than a tennis ball orbiting Earth. Most are fragments of spacecraft lost during launches, including the complete abandoned upper stages of rockets. All are traveling around Earth at speeds of several miles per second. Collisions can be very dangerous, so several teams track the space junk all the time. The Space Shuttle orbiters often have to move out of the way of large pieces of debris.

Back to Earth

Some pieces of space junk fall back to Earth. Many are designed to do so, and burn up completely on reentry into the atmosphere. Sometimes, however, larger pieces make it to the ground. In 1979, a 85-ton disused orbiting laboratory called *Skylab* broke up on reentry, and pieces fell on parts of Australia and in the Indian Ocean. One person has even been struck on the shoulder by a small piece of space junk. In 1997, two heavy parts of a Delta II rocket hit Georgetown, in Texas.

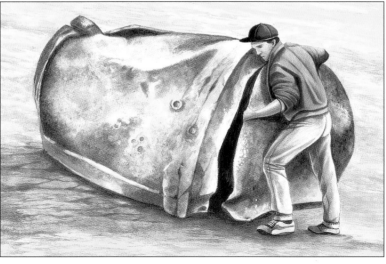

▲ The crumpled booster of the Delta II rocket that fell in Texas in 1997

PROBING SPACE

SPACE EXPLORATION

The best way to find out about a distant object in space, such as another planet, is to go and visit it. It has not yet been possible to send people any farther than the Moon, because it takes months or years to reach the other planets. But robot spacecraft called space probes, which do not need food, drink, or toilets, have seen some of the Solar System's most intriguing and beautiful sights close-up.

Space probes have visited all the planets except Pluto and most of the Solar System's moons, including our own Moon. They have investigated comets and asteroids, and taken close-up pictures of the Sun. There are two main types of space probe mission. In the first, the probe remains in orbit around the planet or moon, or simply flies by, taking photographs and collecting other information. A probe in orbit around a planet can produce detailed maps of the planet's surface over many orbits. In the second type of mission, the space probe plunges down toward the surface of the planet or moon. Sometimes, a probe actually lands on the surface, analyzes the rock, and takes photographs. A space probe receives instructions coded in radio signals sent from scientists on Earth. It sends back radio signals containing information about where it is, as well as the results of any experiments it has carried out and photographs it has taken.

◀ Artist's impression of the *Voyager 2* space probe on its flyby of Jupiter and its moons. *Voyager 2* also flew by planets Saturn, Uranus, and Neptune.

Flyby

A space probe in orbit around another planet is similar to a weather satellite or a remote sensing satellite in orbit around Earth. As well as taking revealing photographs of the planet, it collects useful information about its magnetic field, its atmosphere, and its surface. However, a space probe around another planet has slightly different goals from those of a satellite in Earth orbit. It needs to carry instruments that allow space scientists to work out the composition of the planet (what it is made of) and to hunt for and investigate any moons that are in orbit around it.

A closer look

A space probe that descends into the atmosphere—or even lands on a planet—has a very different view from a space probe in orbit. Normally, it will send information and photographs up to an orbiting probe far above it, so that the orbiter can relay them to Earth. Photographs taken at the surface of another planet are perhaps the most exciting images to come from the exploration of space. Space probes have landed on the Moon, Mars, Venus, and Eros while probes have been dropped into the atmospheres of Jupiter and Venus.

◀ The rover Sojourner on the surface of Mars, in 1997

◀ We now have a good idea of the conditions on Neptune's moon Triton.

▶ Luna 3 took the first photographs of the Moon's far side in 1959.

Moon probes

The first object in space to be visited by space probes was the Moon. Starting in 1959, the Soviet Union and the U.S. sent more than 40 space probes to the Moon. Some flew by, some went into lunar orbit, some crashed, and some landed. The first one, *Luna 1*, was supposed to hit the Moon, but it was traveling too fast, and flew straight past. It is now in orbit around the Sun. In the same year, the probe *Luna 3* took the first-ever photographs of the Moon's far side.

Long-distance communication

The planets are so far away that radio signals sent from Earth take a long time to reach a space probe in orbit or on the surface. So a space probe must be able to make some of its own decisions about where to go and what to photograph. The huge distance from Earth also means that the signals the probe sends back are very weak by the time they reach us. When *Voyager 2* flew by Neptune and its moons, it was 2.8 billion miles (4.5 billion km) away, and signals took more than four hours to reach Earth.

▶ The *Viking* landers failed to find any signs of Martian life.

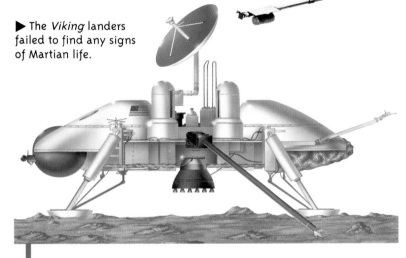

▲ *Mariner 10* is the only space probe that has visited Mercury.

Martian landers

In 1976, two American space probes—*Viking 1* and *Viking 2*— arrived at Mars. Each one consisted of a lander and an orbiter, and both landers made soft landings on the planet. The landers sent back exciting pictures of the Martian surface and sky, and even had long robot arms which scooped up samples of the soil. Chemical laboratories on board analyzed the soil, looking for evidence of life on Mars, and sent information back to scientists on Earth. Meanwhile, the orbiters were busy taking thousands of photographs of the planet from above.

The *Mariner* probes

Between 1962 and 1974, NASA sent a whole series of orbiter and flyby probes called *Mariner* to explore the terrestrial planets. Four of the *Mariners* visited Mars— *Mariner 4* obtained the first close-up images of the Martian surface in 1964. Three Mariners went to Venus—*Mariner 5* flew just 2,400 miles (3,900 km) above its surface in 1967. In 1974, *Mariner 10* also flew by Venus. It went on to become the first probe ever to visit Mercury, and sent back high-quality images of most of the planet's cratered surface.

Out of the Solar System

The most successful space probes ever are *Voyager 1* and *2*. Both traveled to Jupiter (1979) and Saturn (1980 and 1981). *Voyager 2* went on to Uranus (1986) and Neptune (1989). Each *Voyager* carried cameras, spectrometers to test temperatures and compositions of the planets and their moons, and instruments for detecting magnetic fields and cosmic rays— streams of high-energy particles. Both *Voyagers* are now in the outer reaches of the Solar System, way past the orbits of Neptune and Pluto, and are still relaying valuable information.

▲ After it had finished its mission at Neptune, space engineers on Earth instructed *Voyager 2* to turn around and take this view of the planet.

SPACE STATIONS

SPACE EXPLORATION

Orbiting 125 miles (200 km) above Earth's surface is the International Space Station (ISS), which is still under construction. When completed, it will be 260 feet long and 360 feet wide (80 m by 110 m), and will have a mass of about 550 tons (500 tonnes). The ISS is the largest space station built to date.

Space Shuttle missions only last up to 17 days, after which the orbiter and all its crew return to Earth. Astronauts can stay in a space station for much longer periods, with spacecraft bringing additional supplies and replacement crew members from time to time. There are astronauts who have spent several months at a time on space stations. The first space station was *Salyut 1*, a Soviet spacecraft launched in 1971. In 1973, the U.S. sent its first space station, *Skylab*, into orbit. These two spacecraft were followed by several others during the 1970s and 1980s, but many of them had only limited success. However, they did allow spaceflight engineers to learn a great deal about the long-term effects of space travel on the human body, and to find better ways to design living quarters in space. In 1986, the Soviet Union sent up its most successful space station, *Mir*, which remained occupied almost continuously for more than 13 years. According to the International Space Station project leaders, the day the first crew of the ISS arrived at the station, October 31, 2000, was the first day of permanent human occupation of space.

▲ The first U.S. space station, *Skylab*, 270 miles (430 km) above Earth's surface

Skylab

A Saturn V rocket that was left over from the Apollo Moon program launched *Skylab* into orbit in May 1973. The last of three sets of three-person crews left *Skylab* in February 1974. Each mission conducted research on the Sun and the Earth, and included several space walks. The final *Skylab* crew also made the first observations of a comet from space. The *Skylab* spacecraft was 82 feet long and 23 feet wide (25 m by 7 m). In 1979, it went out of control and it plunged into the atmosphere. Some pieces landed on Earth.

▲ Soviets Solovyev and Budarin emerge from a craft supplying space station *Mir*.

Meeting in space

Modern space stations involve international collaboration, with spacecraft from different countries docking (joining together). The first time that this happened was in July 1975, as part of the American and Soviet Apollo-Soyuz Test Project. The astronauts passed through a sealed airlock beween the two spacecraft. The Russian space station *Mir* received astronauts from several different countries, and the ISS is a truly international project, in which 16 nations are taking part.

▲ *Salyut 1*, the world's first space station, in orbit around the Earth

Salyut 1

During the 1960s, the Soviet Union was working on a military space station called *Almaz*. In 1970, the Soviet leader, Leonid Brezhnev, decided to scrap the *Almaz* project and build a civilian (non-military) space station to beat the American *Skylab* project. The result was the world's first space station, *Salyut 1*. It carried several scientific experiments and two telescopes, but its main aim was to learn about long-term visits to space. A total of six *Salyut* space stations were launched, including two military ones.

Mir

Russia's most successful space station —*Mir*—was the first with several modules joined together. The core module was launched in 1986 to an orbit of 242 miles (390 km) high. Six modules were attached to it, five of them carrying scientific experiments or astronomical instruments. The sixth was a docking port for the Space Shuttle orbiter. In 13 years, *Mir* was visited by 11 orbiters. It set many records, including the longest continuous visit to space—Valeri Polyakov spent 438 days on the craft.

▲ Two Russian astronauts carrying out experiments in the core module of *Mir*, the longest-lasting space station.

The way ahead

Missions on the ISS involve up to seven astronauts and last up to six months. Escape vehicles are attached to the space station, so the crew can return to Earth in an emergency. The ISS will have three laboratories for conducting experiments in biology, Earth sciences, physics, and chemistry. Attached to the ISS will be four pallets—experimental setups exposed to space, a large centrifuge—a rapidly spinning device that will be used for research into artificial gravity, and all the usual living quarters and engineering facilities.

▼ The finished ISS will have 43,000 square feet (4,000 sq m) of solar panels.

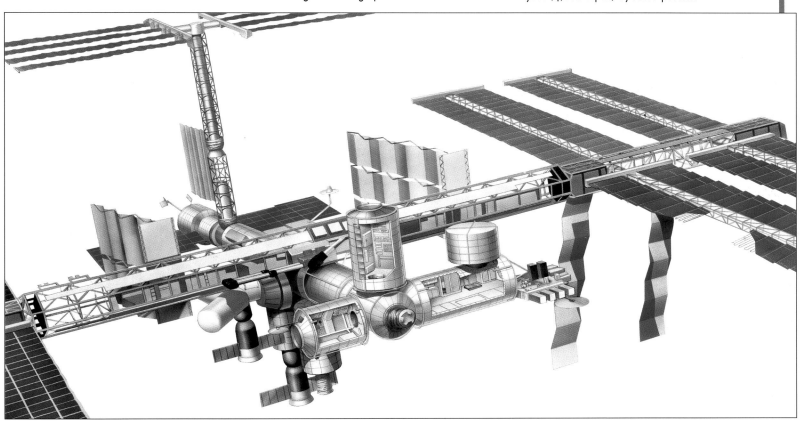

Some ISS research projects

- Tackling disease. Some very important living compounds, from protein molecules to complete cells, can be studied best when they are unaffected by gravity.

- The human body. Long periods in zero gravity allow new studies of the body's organs and systems.

- Technology. Under zero gravity it may be possible to refine purer metals—for example, for use in computer chips.

- Earth-watching. Long-term monitoring provides a global perspective unavailable from the ground with respect to weather, natural features, and pollution.

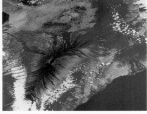

▶ Hawaii seen from the ISS

Construction kit

The first section of the ISS, called Zarya, was put into orbit by a Russian *Proton* rocket in 1998. Other parts are bolted on—a process that will involve more than 40 visits by Space Shuttle orbiters as well as Russian *Proton* and *Soyuz* rockets.

Robot arms are used to maneuver the modules together, and astronauts on space walks make the final adjustments and connect power cables and supply hoses. Inside the ISS, astronauts oversee the construction using a remotely-controlled camera that flies around the ISS looking for faults.

▶ The ISS is visible from Earth because it reflects sunlight.

TIME LINE

BC

About 15,000,000,000 The Big Bang.

About 14,000,000,000 Galaxies (including the Milky Way) form and the first stars start to shine.

4,600,000,000 Formation of the Solar System.

4,000,000,000 End of the heaviest bombardment of the Earth and Moon by Solar System bodies.

3,400,000,000 Date of the earliest fossils so far discovered.

500,000,000 The first vertebrates (animals with a backbone) appear.

225,000,000 and **65,000,000** Mass extinctions due to global climate changes, when many species disappear.

15,000,000 Earliest humans appear.

4007 Origin of the Earth as calculated from Biblical reckoning.

About 3000 Stonehenge construction begins.

Before 2000 The first constellations described by Babylonian astronomers.

250 The Greek astronomer Aristarchus suggests that the Earth and planets orbit the Sun.

129 The Greek astronomer Hipparchus catalogs 1,022 naked-eye stars.

AD

150 The Greek astronomer Ptolemy produces his Earth-centered model of the Solar System.

970 The Persian astronomer Al-Sufi produces an important catalog of more than a thousand stars.

1054 Supernova in the constellation Taurus observed by Chinese astronomers.

1543 The Polish astronomer Nicolaus Copernicus publishes his book suggesting that the planets orbit the Sun.

1570-1600 Danish astronomer Tycho Brahe makes painstaking naked-eye observations of the positions of the planets.

1572 Supernova in the constellation Cassiopeia observed by Tycho Brahe.

1608 The Dutch optician Hans Lippershey invents the refracting telescope.

1609-10 Galileo makes many discoveries with the newly-invented telescope.

1618 Johannes Kepler is the first to develop a modern understanding of orbits.

1633 Galileo is forced by the Church to recant (deny) his theory that the planets orbit the Sun.

1647 The first complete map of the Moon published by the Danish astronomer John Hevel (also known as Hevelius).

1668 Isaac Newton constructs the first reflecting telescope.

1687 Isaac Newton publishes his Law of Universal Gravitation.

1725 Publication of the first telescopic star catalog, by the English Astronomer Royal John Flamsteed.

1758 Halley's Comet makes its return as predicted by Edmund Halley.

1781 William Herschel discovers Uranus (March 13).

1801 Italian astronomer Giuseppe Piazzi is first to see an asteroid, Ceres (January 1).

1833 A great meteor storm (the Leonids) recorded in the U.S. (November 11). Other great storms seen in 1866, 1966, and 1999.

1838 The distance to a nearby star measured by the German astronomer Friedrich Wilhelm Bessel.

1840 The first photograph of the Moon taken by the American astronomer John William Draper.

1846 Discovery of Neptune (September 23).

1859 The German chemists Robert Bunsen and Gustav Kirchoff discover that the spectrum of each element shows a different pattern of lines.

1877 Giovanni Schiaparelli reports that he detects "canals" on Mars.

1903 A Soviet science teacher, Konstantin Ziolkovsky, writes a pamphlet describing a rocket-propelled spacecraft.

1908 A small asteroid explodes over Siberia (June 30).

1912 Publication of the Hertzsprung-Russell diagram, which shows how stars can be divided into different groups.

1915 Albert Einstein publishes his General Theory of Relativity, establishing our modern understanding of gravity.

1926 Edwin Hubble divides galaxies into spiral, elliptical, and irregular types.

1926 American scientist Robert Goddard launches the world's first liquid-fuel rocket (March 16).

1928 Edwin Hubble announces that distant galaxies are moving away at high speeds.

1930 Pluto is discovered by Clyde Tombaugh (March 13).

1930 The American radio enthusiast Grote Reber first observes radio waves from space.

1948 U.S. researchers fire a two-stage rocket to a height of 79 miles (127 km) on May 13. In 1949, another goes to 244 miles (393 km).

1948 The Hale reflecting telescope with a 17-foot (5-m) mirror, is finished on Mount Palomar, CA.

1950 Cape Canaveral established as a rocket-launching site.

1957 The first artificial satellite, *Sputnik 1*, is launched by the Soviet Union (October 4).

1958 The USA's first satellite, *Explorer 1*, discovers that the Earth is surrounded by belts of particles sent out by the Sun.

1959 The first man-made object reaches a place other than Earth when the Soviet probe *Luna 3* hits the Moon (September 15).

1961 The first crewed orbit of the Earth is made by the Soviet astronaut Yuri Gagarin (April 12).

1961 Alan Shepard becomes the first American in space (May 5) when he is launched in a *Mercury* capsule.

1963 Quasars are discovered to be very bright and distant galaxies.

1964 Arno Penzias and Robert Wilson discover faint radiation left over from the Big Bang.

1969 *Apollo 11* lands people on the Moon (July 20).

1973 The U.S. *Skylab* space station launched (May 14).

1982 Successful trial flight of the Space Shuttle *Columbia* (April 12).

1986 *Challenger* Shuttle tragedy, when seven astronauts die (January 28).

1986 The first part of the Soviet *Mir* space station launched (February 20).

1990 Launch of the Hubble Space Telescope (April 24).

1991 The 33-foot (10-m) Keck reflecting telescope on Mauna Kea, Hawaii, comes into use.

1998 The first part of the International Space Station launched (November 20).

2001 *NEAR Shoemaker* lands on the asteroid Eros (February 12).

GLOSSARY

asteroids Also called minor planets. Small, rocky objects—between a few yards and 600 miles across—that orbit the Sun. Most asteroids are found between the orbits of Mars and Jupiter.

astronomer A scientist who specializes in making observations of space.

Astronomical Unit The average distance between the Earth and the Sun—about 93 million miles (150m km).

atmosphere A layer of gases around a planet or moon. The gas giant planets have a very deep atmosphere, but atmospheres of the terrestrial planets are much thinner.

atom The tiny basic building block of matter. Atoms consist of electrically charged particles called nuclei and electrons.

Big Bang According to modern cosmology, the moment at which time and space came into existence, about 15 billion years ago.

binary star Two stars close together, in orbit around each other, which appear as one star to the naked eye. (See also double star; eclipsing binary.)

black hole A body whose gravitational field is so strong that light cannot escape from it. A black hole forms from a very massive star at the end of its life, or in the center of a galaxy.

CCD Charge-Coupled Device; an electronic chip used for electronic imaging, consisting of thousands of tiny light-sensitive pixels.

celestial sphere An imaginary sphere carrying the stars, planets, and other celestial objects, which appears to rotate around the Earth once a day.

Cepheid variable A variable star that astronomers use for distance measurement.

comet A Solar System object in an elongated orbit that gives off clouds of gas and dust at its nearest approach to the Sun.

constellation A pattern of stars named after a real or imaginary object or person.

corona The Sun's outer atmosphere, visible during a total solar eclipse.

cosmic background radiation A faint signal of radio waves coming from every direction of space that is the radiation left over from the Big Bang.

cosmologist A space scientist who is concerned with the nature of the Universe as a whole, including trying to find out how it began and how it will end.

crater A mark on the surface of a terrestrial planet or rocky moon made by

the impact of an asteroid or large meteorite. Planets or moons with only a thin atmosphere, or no atmosphere at all, are most heavily cratered.

dark matter Invisible material believed to make up most of the mass of the Universe. Space scientists do not know what dark matter is, but they know it must be there because of the gravitational influence.

double star Any pair of stars that look very close together in the sky. Most double stars are only visible as doubles through a telescope. Binary stars are close together in space, but line-of-sight doubles only appear to lie close together in the sky.

eclipsing binary A type of binary star, in which one star, passing in front of the other, regularly causes it to grow dimmer as seen from Earth.

ecliptic plane The imaginary "race track" on which all the planets orbit the Sun.

electromagnetic radiation Energy emitted by certain objects that travels at the speed of light. Hot objects, like stars, emit electromagnetic radiation across a wide spectrum—from radio waves through visible light to X-rays and gamma rays.

electrons Tiny particles that surround the nucleus in an atom.

energetic galaxy A galaxy with a powerful energy source at its center. Space scientists think that most energetic galaxies contain massive black holes.

galaxy A huge system of stars, gas, dust, and dark matter. Our Solar System is in the Milky Way Galaxy.

gamma rays A type of electromagnetic radiation emitted by high-energy processes, like nuclear reactions, or from extremely hot objects.

gas giant Any of the planets Jupiter, Saturn, Uranus, and Neptune, which are made largely of gas.

geocentric "Earth-centered"—in particular, the old idea that the Sun and planets all move around the Earth.

geostationary (geosynchronous) orbit An orbit at a distance of about 22,200 miles (35,700 km) above the Earth. Satellites at this distance make a full orbit in one day, so stay above a single point on Earth.

giant molecular cloud A mixture of gas and solid particles, a dense region of the interstellar medium from which stars form.

giant star A star that has expanded greatly as it nears the end of its life.

globular cluster A group of up to a million old stars that are all the same age.

gravitation A force that acts between all matter in the Universe. It pulls everything together, giving weight to things on Earth and enabling objects to orbit each other.

greenhouse effect The trapping of heat from the Sun by carbon dioxide or other gases in a planet's atmosphere.

heliocentric "Sun-centered"—the modern idea of the Solar System, first published by Polish astronomer Nicolaus Copernicus.

helium A chemical element that is very common in the Universe. Helium is made from hydrogen during nuclear fusion in the centers of stars. At room temperature, helium is a gas.

Hertzsprung-Russell (H-R) diagram A way of sorting out stars into different types as a graph that shows luminosity on one axis and temperature on the other. Main sequence stars appear as a diagonal band across the graph.

Hubble constant A measure of the rate at which the Universe is expanding, in units of kilometers per second per megaparsec.

hydrogen The most abundant chemical element in the Universe. All the hydrogen that exists was created in the early stages of the Universe. Inside stars, hydrogen is changed into helium by nuclear fusion. At room temperature, hydrogen is a gas.

inferior planet A planet that is always closer to the Sun than Earth is.

infrared radiation A type of electromagnetic radiation that is emitted by warm objects, including human bodies. It is invisible to human eyes.

interstellar medium Extremely thin gas and dust particles that fill the space between the stars.

Kuiper Belt A zone extending outward beyond planet Neptune, where a group of large asteroids orbits the Sun.

light-year The distance light travels in a year—about 6 trillion miles (9.5 trillion km).

luminosity The amount of light given out by an object each second. If two stars are at the same distance from Earth, but have different luminosities, the more luminous one will appear brighter. (See magnitude.)

lunar eclipse When the Moon passes through Earth's shadow. During a lunar eclipse, the Moon becomes reddish-brown or disappears completely for up to an hour.

Magellanic Clouds Two satellite galaxies of the Milky Way Galaxy.

magnitude A measure of the brightness of a star or planet. The brightest star in the night sky is Sirius, with a magnitude of -1.4. The dimmest object visible to the naked eye has a magnitude of about +6.

main sequence The stable, middle part of a star's lifetime, when it converts hydrogen to helium at its core, by nuclear fusion.

maria "Seas"—the word used to describe the dark lava plains on the Moon.

megaparsec One million parsecs—3.26 million light-years.

metallic hydrogen A strange form of matter, made from hydrogen, found around the cores of gas giant planets. It behaves as a liquid, but is more dense than a solid.

meteor The streak of light seen when a meteoroid burns up in the atmosphere.

meteorite The solid body that reaches the ground when a large meteoroid does not burn up completely in the atmosphere.

meteoroid A solid object smaller than a few yards across in orbit around the Sun.

microgravity The near weightless conditions experienced by astronauts in orbit around the Earth. In a perfectly circular orbit, astronauts experience total weightlessness, called zero gravity.

Milky Way Galaxy Our own galaxy. In some parts of the night sky, the center of the galaxy appears as a hazy band of light called the Milky Way.

nebula A cloud of gas and dust that is visible from Earth, normally because light from nearby stars illuminates it. Some nebulas are the birthplaces of stars; others are made from the gas and dust thrown off by a dying star.

neutron star An extremely dense remnant of a dying star, made of atomic nuclei crushed together. (See pulsar).

nuclear fusion A reaction in which nuclei —the tiny central parts of atoms—of one element are crushed together and merge to form a different element. Inside stars, hydrogen nuclei become helium nuclei by nuclear fusion.

nucleus (plural **nuclei**) The central part of an atom. At high temperatures or low pressures, nuclei exist on their own, without the electrons that normally surround them.

Oort cloud A suggested "shell" of comets in the outer Solar System, hundreds of times more distant than Pluto.

orbit The path through space followed by an astronomical object or a spacecraft as it moves around another object.

parallax The shift of a nearby star against the background of more distant stars, as seen several months apart. Parallax is used to work out the distances of nearby stars.

parsec A distance of 3.26 light-years.

phases The part of the illuminated half of the Moon as seen from Earth. The phases change gradually over each month from new moon to full moon and back again. The inferior planets, Mercury and Venus, also show phases.

planet Any of the nine large objects in orbit around the Sun. Five of the planets, including Earth, are rocky, while the other four are gas giants.

planetary nebula A cloud of gas puffed out by a dying star. (See nebula.)

plasma A form of matter, which occurs at high temperature or very low pressure, in which electrons are separated from nuclei. Stars are made from plasma.

prominence A fountain of glowing hydrogen rising from the Sun's surface.

protostar The early stage in the lifetime of a star, formed by the collapse of a giant molecular cloud due to gravity.

pulsar A spinning neutron star that sends out a rotating beam of radio waves like a lighthouse.

quasar A rare type of energetic galaxy with a very bright center. Quasars are the most distant objects known.

radio waves A form of electromagnetic radiation, invisible to human eyes, that is produced by a variety of physical processes, including the movement of electrons inside a galaxy. Astronomers detect radio waves using a radio telescope.

red shift The change in position— toward the red end of the spectrum—of lines in the spectrum of a distant galaxy that is moving away from us at high speed.

ring system Millions of small particles in orbit around a gas giant. Planet Saturn has the most spectacular ring system.

satellite Any object that is in orbit around another. The Moon is Earth's only natural satellite, but there are thousands of artificial satellites—spacecraft launched from Earth.

SETI Abbreviation for "search for extraterrestrial intelligence," carried on with radio telescopes.

solar eclipse The passage of the Moon in front of the Sun, blocking its light in small regions on Earth.

Solar System The planets, the asteroids, meteoroids, comets, the Kuiper Belt, and the Oort Cloud, all in orbit around our star, the Sun.

solar wind A continuous stream of tiny particles from the Sun that "blow" at high speed through the Solar System.

space scientist A scientist who studies space. (See astronomer; cosmologist.)

spectroscopy The science that enables astronomers to work out the temperatures and compositions of objects in space by examining the spectrum of light coming from them.

spectrum A band of all the colors—from red through to blue—that make up white light. The electromagnetic spectrum extends much farther to include other types of electromagnetic radiation.

star A huge ball of plasma. Except for the Sun, our nearest star, the stars that are visible from Earth appear as tiny points of light because they are so far away.

Sun The nearest star, and the object around which all the objects of the Solar System orbit.

supercluster An enormous cluster containing smaller clusters of galaxies.

supergiant star An extra-large giant star.

superior planet A planet that is always farther away from the Sun than the Earth is.

supernova An exploding supergiant star. They are so bright that astronomers sometimes observe them in other galaxies.

terrestrial "Earthlike"—the planets Mercury, Venus, Earth, and Mars are called the terrestrial planets.

ultraviolet radiation A form of electromagnetic radiation that is invisible to the human eye, just beyond the blue end of the visible light spectrum.

variable star A star that changes in brightness. (See eclipsing binary; Cepheid variable.)

visible light Electromagnetic radiation that is visible to the human eye—all the colors of the spectrum, from red to blue.

white dwarf star A dying star that has lost most of its original material. The Sun will eventually become a white dwarf.

X-rays Electromagnetic radiation that is invisible to the eye. It is produced by high-energy processes and very hot objects.

zodiac A band around the celestial sphere centered on the ecliptic. It contains the Zodiacal Constellations—the ones through which the Sun passes in a year.

INDEX

Abbreviations: t-top, m-middle, b-bottom, r-right, l-left, c-center

Artwork credits: 13bl, 17tr—Geoff Ball. 71br—John Butler. 11ml, 21mr, 40br—Carol Daniel. 6/7, 43mr, 43tr, 56bl—Piers Harper. 72tr—Colin Howard. 29bl, 49r, 56br, 57mr—Mike Lacey. 5ml, 9ml, 18mr, 36bl, 38bl, 46t—Alex Pang. 10t, 10ml—Stan Peach. 8, 11mr, 12t, 12b, 13mr, 21t, 21mb, 21bl, 27bl, 29br, 34bl, 39tl, 39bm, 40bl, 41bl, 43br, 44tr, 45br, 45bl, 47mr, 52m, 62mr, 63t—Stephen Sweet. 19br—Catherine Ward. 28bl, 33br, 56ml, 58/59—Mike Taylor.

Photograph credits: 1, 2, 3bl, 3br, 9br, 13tl, 19c, 22ml, 24bl, 25c, 25bl, 26mr, 30tr, 31mr, 34tr, 35tr, 36mr, 37tr, 38tr, 39tr, 39bl, 42m, 45mr, 46bl, 47mr, 51tl, 53tl, 53mr, 54bl, 55br both, 57tl, 64mr, 65t, 65rt both, 66tr, 66mr, 67c, 67tr, 68bl, 69br, 73tl, 73tr, 73br, 74tr, 75bl—Corbis/RoyaltyFree. 3ml, 15tl, 25tr—Dennis di Cicco/CORBIS. 3tr, 49m—NASA/SAO/CXC/Galaxy. 4bl, 27ml, 33ml, 65rb, 72b, 75br—Stockbyte. 5r, 15bl, 20bl, 23br, 37mr all, 41tr, 41ml, 57br, 66b, 67br, 68tr, 68tl, 69br, 73mr, 74mr—CORBIS. 10mr—Adam Woolfitt/CORBIS. 14b—Roger Ressmeyer/CORBIS. 17bl—Francisco Diego/Galaxy. 17mr—Richard Wainscoat/Galaxy. 17br, 22tr, 49b—Robin Scagell/Galaxy. 17c—Hellemans and Verschraegen. 18bl, 20mr, 22br, 31tl, 33c, 59bl—NASA/Galaxy. 19tl—Richard Smith/Galaxy. 3mr, 19tr, 31br, 61tr, 61tl, 61ml, 61bl, 61mr, 63ml, 63mr, 64br, 65ml, 69tl, 70tl, 70mr, 71ml, 75t—Genesis Photo Library. 19b, 63br—Universal (Courtesy Kobal). 28tr—Bob Krist/CORBIS. 31ml—NASA/CORBIS. 27t, 27tr, 32ml, 35ml, 37ml all, 39mr both, 52b, 54tr, 67bl both—NASA. 32br—Jonathon Blair/ CORBIS. 41, 48tr, 51ml, 69bl, 74bl—NASA/Roger Ressmeyer/CORBIS. 42b—STScl/Galaxy. 43tr—Clyde Tombaugh. 45—Aaron Horowitz/CORBIS. 47bl—STScl/AURA. 50b—NASA/Hubble Heritage Team. 57ml—Super-Kamiokande. 59mr, 60bl, 63c, 61br—Kobal. 67tl—NMPFT/Science & Society Picture Library.